A Pilgrim's Guide to
OBERAMMERGAU
AND ITS PASSION PLAY
By Raymond Goodburn
Contributions and Editorial – Andrew Houseley

Pilgrim Book Services Limited

Published by Pilgrim Book Services Ltd., registered at 21 Birchwood Drive, Rushmere St Andrew, Ipswich, Suffolk IP5 1EB, United Kingdom.

www.pilgrimbooks.com

Sixth Edition 2019

Typesetting and design by Winmark Graphics.

Cover design by Ivan Yonov; original cover designs by Fielding Design.

Maps by Kevin Baverstock. Data available under the Open Database License. © OpenStreetMap contributors.

MIX
Paper from
responsible sources

FSC
www.fsc.org   FSC® C006671

Printed in the United Kingdom by Healeys.

The publishers and author are grateful for the assistance of the following.
Gemeinde Oberammergau, in particular the Mayor, Arno Nunn.
Oberammergau Kultur, in particular Frederik Mayet, Walter Rutz and Franziska Zankl.
The Creative Team of the Passion Play: Christian Stückl, Abdul Karaca and Markus Zwink.
Ammergau Alpen Tourismus: Florian Hoffrohne, Nicole Richter and Ute Oberhauser.
Rothenburg Tourismus Service, in particular Dr Jörg Christöffler.

Cover picture and title page:
Jesus prays to the Father at the Mount of Olives. © Oberammergau Passion Play 2020

2

CONTENTS

List of Maps

PREFACE

To come to Oberammergau and see the world famous Passion Play is an experience many people want to achieve at least once in their lifetime. For many, attending the Passion Play will be a faith- and life-affirming event. There are several characteristics that go into making the 'Oberammergau Experience' unique and so memorable. Performing a play telling of the betrayal, trial, suffering, execution and resurrection of Jesus Christ is a centuries-old tradition, however no performance has survived as long, through the ages, as that of this village in Upper Bavaria. It was begun as a desperate act of faith to ward off death from the plague, apparently successfully. But in these modern times with so many distractions and where it seems science explains everything, it is incredible that the Vow of the villagers has lived on through so many generations. Over that time, what began as a simple performance has evolved into an amazingly high quality presentation of acting, music and staging – and hospitality – an amateur production involving almost the entire community. The sheer dedication of villagers to the arts and skills required is almost impossible to find in such a small community anywhere else in the world. The fame of the Passion Play has spread throughout the world, particularly where English is the first language, and has attracted visitors in high numbers – and this is despite the five-hour-long performance being spoken in German.

All of this is carried out in one of Europe's most scenic locations, and Oberammergau has several iconic features of landscape and architecture to help place the experience indelibly into the memory. The necessarily short time visitors have in the Oberammergau area in order to make way for the next attendees of the play, allows a longer holiday to some of the most glorious parts of Europe, or to venture even further afield.

Through this book, we want visitors to come to a greater understanding of all of these elements, to prepare well for their short visit to the area, to follow the action on stage, to also enjoy their visits to some of the attractions of the wider area, and determine to make a return visit in the not too distant future. Through Ray Goodburn in particular, I am confident that you are in good hands. May this book enhance your own 'Oberammergau Experience'.

Andrew Houseley

Frescoed house in the village

THE SETTING AND
THE STORY

Nestling among the Bavarian Alps in the Ammergau Valley is the delightful village of Oberammergau, with a population of about 5,400. The Ammergau Valley has been an important communications route for centuries. Indeed, research suggests traces of settlements in the upper Ammer valley dating back to Celtic times. During the Roman period it lay on the military route from Verona to Augsburg and in common with most of the passable routes across the Alps it has been fought over time and again. Eventually the Ammergau region became the centre of a far-reaching area and from the ninth century onwards it was the religious focal point for the entire valley. Subsequently it was in the hands of many different rulers, but most importantly as part of the lands of the Dukes of Bavaria, culminating with the rule of the 'mad' King Ludwig II, a close friend of Richard Wagner and builder of the nearby 'fairy-tale' castles.

The village stands more than 800 metres above sea level in a valley almost totally surrounded by mountains. From a southerly and easterly direction it is approached by a road which winds its way up from the autobahn between Munich and Garmisch-Partenkirchen. The other main road takes a northerly direction, following the river Ammer through the 'twin' village of Unterammergau, and then to Schongau and north towards Augsburg.

Coming from the direction of Garmisch the road passes through the village of Ettal, with its huge monastery and fine church built in 1330. Oberammergau was administered from here for many years, and the monastery and its incumbents have always had a great influence on the Passion Play, as we shall see later. Together with its fellow monastic institutions at Rottenbuch and Steingaden, Ettal forms a geographical triangle, in the southern corner of which lies Oberammergau.

In its trade route days, the people of the village made a good living from providing transport and lodgings for the traveller. But in winter it was a very different story. Once the snows arrived, those who lived in the mountains could not move far from their homes and so they developed the art of woodcarving, a skill for which the village is still renowned today. They would spend the winter carving

The view from the Laber

toys, religious figures and household utensils, and when summer came they would set off to peddle their wares in the surrounding villages and beyond, carrying their goods on a large wooden frame slung over their backs. In the centre of the village there used to be a wooden representation of just such a pedlar, but unfortunately this became so damaged by the ravages of the climate that it had to be taken down. The nearest approximation you can find these days is on the road out to Ettal where eventually, on the right, you will see a pedlar modelled in stone! But in the winter even he is encased in wood to protect him from the winter frosts and snows.

Of the surrounding mountains, two in particular stand out. The Laber, on the eastern edge of Oberammergau, is 1,684m high, and can be ascended from the village by cable-car. On the southern edge of the village is the Kofel (1,342m), a sugar-loaf-shaped mountain with a great cross on its peak. This is often used as a symbol of the village and it is on the slopes of the Kofel that many of the traditional festivities of the village take place, such as the torchlight procession celebrating the birthday of King Ludwig II.

But what makes Oberammergau so special? The answer, of course, lies in events in the first part of the 17th century. From 1618–1648 the 'Thirty Years War' engulfed much of Europe. It began as a religious conflict between Protestants and Catholics, for even though the Protestant Reformation had happened a century earlier, the two groups had not yet learned to live amicably together. However, it gradually developed into a general war across Europe for reasons not necessarily related to religion, and in its wake brought widespread famine and disease which spread like wildfire across the continent and devastated large parts of Germany. In 1631, the Protestant army of the Swedish King, Gustav-Adolf, had heavily defeated the Catholics at Breitenfeld, and went on to take Würzburg and Munich. The whole of Bavaria was being ravaged by gangs of marauding soldiers who, being unpaid and underfed, went on orgies of rape and pillage wherever they could, so helping to spread the plague or 'black death', which claimed more than a million lives through Saxony and Bavaria alone as towns and villages were devastated.

For quite some time the small village of Oberammergau managed to keep the plague at bay, mainly because of its favourable position, surrounded by mountains and accessible only in the summer months. In addition, there was a strictly enforced quarantine, with guards severely restricting the movement of people in and out of the village, particularly preventing access to strangers. These measures meant that the villagers stayed free of the disease – until one night, an

Fresco showing the first play

inhabitant of Oberammergau named Kaspar Schisler, who had been living and working away from home at Eschenlohe, evaded the guards under cover of darkness and crept back into the village to visit his family and share in the festival marking the dedication of the church. Unwittingly he brought the plague with him from Eschenlohe, only a few miles away and a community which had already succumbed to the disease, resulting not only in his own death and the deaths of his wife and children, but within months 84 adults in Oberammergau are known to have died.

In those days little enough was known about the cause of such diseases and out of ignorance it was all too easy to concoct remarkable stories in an attempt to explain them. There were those, for example, who attributed such a disaster to the hand of God and believed that it was sent as a punishment. Consequently, it was thought that some form of penitence and expression of faith taken in a collective and public way might avert any further wrath of the Almighty. So it was that in July 1633 the Village Council, in a desperate act of faith, summoned those who were able to meet in the church and there, before the altar, they made a solemn vow to perform, every tenth year, a play of the Saviour's suffering and death, if God would deliver them from the disease. From that day, it is recorded, no one else in

Oberammergau died from the disease.

The performance of a Passion Play in fulfilment of a vow is not unique, but in Oberammergau it has a remarkable record of survival and continuity, despite wars, military occupations, and even an anti-religious edict during a period of secularisation. It is this persistence which has given the Oberammergau Play its prominence among all other such productions, as well as according it world-wide renown. The first performance was given at Pentecost in 1634 by some sixty or seventy performers, on a stage erected over the graves of the plague victims. From then on it was repeated every ten years until 1674, when it was decided to bring the performance to the beginning of each decade. Only twice did the Play not take place – in 1770 when there was a ban on passion plays, and in 1940 due to World War II. Such is the ongoing determination to honour the original vow.

It is strange to reflect that but for the Thirty Years War and the accompanying plague, the Oberammergau Passion Play might well have never happened, and that in subsequent centuries any fame for the village would have been much more limited, centred on the quality of its woodcarving and its association with King Ludwig II. But whether you visit Oberammergau to attend the Play, or in non-Play years just as a tourist, there is no escaping what it means to the village. The village lives and breathes the Play, for the Play is Oberammergau and Oberammergau is the Play.

A TOUR OF
THE VILLAGE

Whether you are visiting Oberammergau to see the Play or whether you are here out of season, so to speak, there is much of interest and beauty in the village. Those who come to see the Passion Play will probably come as part of a wider tour, whether organised through a company or independently, and at the most will spend two nights in the village, perhaps arriving the night before the performance and leaving the morning after. Given the new timings for the Play (which were inaugurated in 2010), afternoon and evening rather than morning and afternoon, that should allow most of the morning before the performance to discover something of the village and to do a little shopping – as well as have lunch. Hopefully even this brief acquaintance with Oberammergau might act as a stimulus to return another year and stay for longer.

The village does in fact make an excellent centre for a holiday at any time of the year, and most years welcomes about 70,000 visitors. All being well, this chapter and a subsequent one about what can be seen in the surrounding area will confirm that. For walkers, there are many paths and trails, clearly signed, whether you want a mountain hike or a gentle stroll through the valleys. Keen cyclists will also find several cycle tracks. In addition, there are excellent winter-sports facilities, and in non-Play years there may well be as many visitors here in the winter as in the summer, though that, of course, greatly depends on the amount of snowfall which these days can be somewhat unpredictable. There are ski-lifts, a chair-lift to the Kolbensattel and the cable-car to the Laber, mentioned in the previous chapter. Furthermore, several good ski runs exist and the area is also popular for cross-country runs into the Grasswang valley. One famous run, 'In the footsteps of King Ludwig,' is just over 30 miles long and races are held each year during the first weekend in February. Then, of course, there are the Olympic standard facilities of Garmisch-Partenkirchen, which is only about 19 km away.

However brief or long your visit, and irrespective of whether you stay summer or winter, one of the first things to strike you about Oberammergau will be the decorated **frescoes** on many of the buildings, and these are the main visual

Pilate's house

attraction of the village. Although this technique is quite common throughout Bavaria and in parts of the Austrian Tyrol, it is nowhere quite as distinctive as it is in Oberammergau and as you walk around the village you will see many buildings with painted façades depicting religious themes, rural scenes or fairy tales. In German these frescoes are known as *lüftmalerei*, or 'air painting.' This technique seems to have originated from the practice of decorating baroque façades in Italy and Southern Germany. It was only in the 18th century that it became popular in the foothills of the Alps, where wealthy traders and craftsmen displayed something of their prosperity by painting opulent façades. This particular art form is accomplished by applying mineral-based water colours to wet, freshly laid plaster. As the colours dry they become fixed and insoluble to water. It is a version of the *trompe l'oeil* effect, which tricks the eye into believing that what is basically a two-dimensional painting is in fact three-dimensional.

One explanation for the name of the technique stems from the need to work quickly in the open air (*lüft*). However, an alternative interpretation much favoured in Oberammergau is that it is taken from the name of the house in the village, 'Zum Lüftl,' owned by Franz Seraph Zwink (1748–1792) who was a master of this skill and much of his craft can be seen around the village. Some of his finest examples (1784) are on the building known as **Pilate's House**, where from the garden side you can see a representation of Jesus being condemned by Pilate. As you look around the exterior, the paintings seem to jump out at you with a remarkable 3-D effect. Note, for example, how realistic the spiral staircase looks. While you are here a visit inside is also highly recommended, because you will have an opportunity, normally in the afternoon, to watch various people at work demonstrating their crafts and to ask them questions. There is also a shop where you can purchase handicrafts from woodcarving to *verre églomisé* paintings (see pages 16–17) to pottery, all made by members of the studio.

Before moving on from the *lüftmalerei*, another building of note is the **Hansel and Gretel House**, which stands on the edge of the village along *Ettaler Strasse*, the road out towards Ettal. You will be able to recognise many of the nursery rhyme characters – Puss in Boots, Rumpelstiltskin and many more.

Woodcarving is a long-established skill and still today there are approximately 60 woodcarvers in the village. As you stroll around you will discover many of the shops and workshops dedicated to this special skill. The roots of the craft go back to the Middle Ages, and there is a manuscript which describes how the monks from Rottenbuch brought 'the Ammergau art of carving small household goods out

Hansel and Gretel house

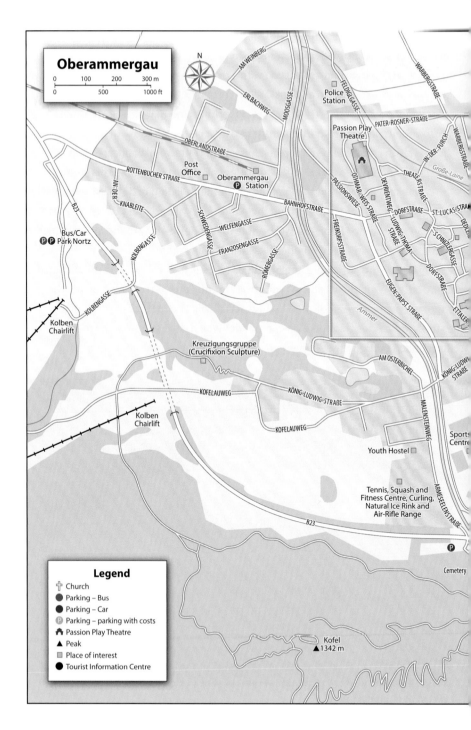

Oberammergau

0 100 200 300 m
0   500   1000 ft

N

AM WEINBERG
ERLBACHWEG
MOOSGASSE
FELDIGGASSE
Police Station
WARBERGSTRAßE
PATER-ROSNER-STRAßE
Passion Play Theatre
IN-DER-FURCH
WARBERGSTRAße
OBERLANDSTRAßE
Post Office
Oberammergau Station
THEATERSTRAße
Große-Laine
ROTTENBUCHER STRAße
OTHMAR-WEIS-STRAßE
PASSIONSWIESE
DER-RIENTWEG
LUDWIG-THOMA-STRAßE
DORFSTRAße
ST.-LUCAS-STRA
AN-DER-
KNABLEITE
BAHNHOFSTRAße
FREIKORPSSTRAße
DEDL
B23
SCHWEDENGASSE
WELFENGASSE
DORFSTRAße
SCHNITZLERGASSE
Bus/Car Park Nortz
KOLBENGASSE
FRANZOSENGASSE
RÖMERGASSE
EUGEN-PAPST STRAße
DORFSTRAße
ETTALER
KOLBENGASSE
Kolben Chairlift
Ammer
Kreuzigungsgruppe (Crucifixion Sculpture)
AM OSTERBICHEL
KÖNIG-LUDWI
STRAße
KOFELAUWEG
KÖNIG-LUDWIG-STRAßE
Kolben Chairlift
KOFELAUWEG
MALENSTEINWEG
Sports Centr
Youth Hostel
Tennis, Squash and Fitness Centre, Curling, Natural Ice Rink and Air-Rifle Range
ARMESEELENSTRAße
B23

Cemetery

Legend

✝ Church
● Parking – Bus
● Parking – Car
Ⓟ Parking – parking with costs
♞ Passion Play Theatre
▲ Peak
◻ Place of interest
● Tourist Information Centre

Kofel
▲1342 m

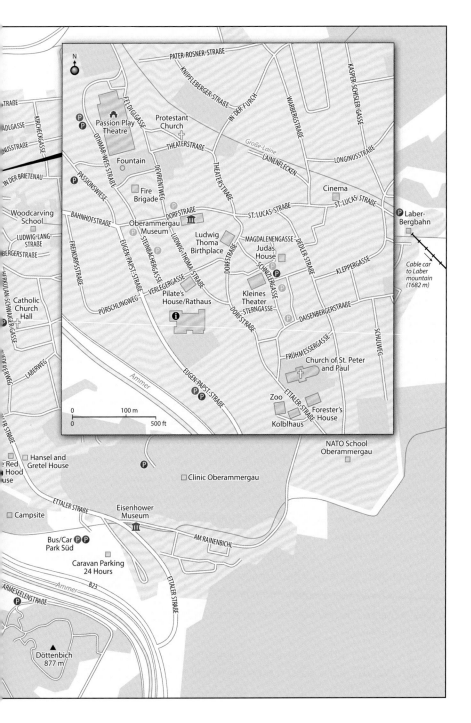

of wood' to the area of Berchtesgaden. In 1520 a traveller from Florence praised the quality of the Oberammergau carvings and in 1563 the Ammergauer carvers received their own Handicrafts Code from the Abbot of Ettal. Initially most of the carvings were sold locally, but by the 18th century many distribution houses were set up with branches all over Europe. From these locations travelling salesmen took on the responsibility of selling the goods from door to door.

Several carvers have their studios open to view and you can sometimes see them at work, with the possibility of purchasing the results. If you are attending the Play you may well recognise some of them as actors. Whilst the quality of the carving does vary and acknowledging, too, that some of it may not be to your taste, nevertheless nearly all the examples on display will have been carved by hand in the village, not machine turned and imported. It follows, therefore, that they will not be cheap. As you wander around the village you will certainly find no shortage of shops displaying and selling goods carved from wood. Also, on Ludwig Lang Strasse, on the road towards the cable-car station, there is a well-known, state run training college for wood carving with an international reputation and this is sometimes open to the public.

If time permits a visit to the **museum** should not be missed. This was built between 1904 and 1906 by the architect Franz Zell from Munich, on the order of Guido Lang (1865–1921), the distributor of wood carved goods. Given the importance of woodcarving in the village, it is not surprising that much of the Museum's display relates to this art. There are crucifixes, figures of saints, needle cases and paperweights created out of maple or fruit-tree wood, all dating from the mid-18th to the late 19th century and all demonstrating the richness of the woodcarver's craft. Moreover, using mainly spruce (but sometimes lime wood), the production of toys displays another characteristic of the area. There are dolls, soldiers, fortresses, wagons and carts, mail-coach drivers and travellers, coachmen and riders.

A further tradition, also dating back to the 18th century, is the carving of Christmas cribs. Prior to this, such nativity scenes had been made primarily from paper and cloth, but in 1760 the woodcarvers created a nativity for their parish church and for several decades continued to re-model it, with Ludwig himself being a great admirer. This crib is extremely precious and the highlight of the crib display on the ground floor.

Along with the various examples of woodcarving, there is also a display of *verre églomisé*, 'Worlds behind glass,' most easily described as 'glass engraved on the back and covered by unfired painting.' This was a style of painting which developed

The parish church's marvellously ornate interior in white and gold

during the 18th century in the regions of Murnau and Oberammergau and which subsequently became a much-cultivated craft. Although the Museum already had a notable exhibition of this art form, in 1955 the authorities acquired a large part of the important collection of *verre églomisé* belonging to Johann Krotz, a master brewer from nearby Murnau, who by the end of the 19th century had amassed more than a thousand examples.

If you are interested in visiting the museum (normally open from mid April to October, Tuesday to Sunday) during your stay in Oberammergau, you may find it helpful to know that from time to time, in addition to its regular displays, the museum also hosts special exhibitions.

The **parish church** is dedicated to the Blessed Virgin Mary and the apostles Peter and Paul. It was built between 1736 and 1742 and is a fine example of the Rococo period with a marvellously ornate interior in white and gold. Prior to this present building there had been other churches in the village – first a simple wooden one, in common with churches in the area, then a Romanesque stone one during the Middle Ages, followed by a Gothic one up until the beginning of the 18th Century. As this building was by then beginning to show considerable damage, almost to the point of being beyond repair, it was decided to construct a new one. There is, as you would expect, some fine carving as well as ceiling paintings, and all the various elements combine to create a wonderfully light atmosphere.

Matthäus Günther, an extremely gifted and much respected Rococo painter, and Franz Seraph Zwink from the village, were responsible for many of the frescoes, having been brought in by Joseph Schmuzer, one of the greatest Bavarian Rococo architects, who already had a considerable reputation as a master builder. Much of the stucco work was carried out by Schmuzer's son, Franz Xavier Schmuzer, but in all probability based on his father's plans. Though they may look as if they are created from marble, all the altars and statues are carved from wood. If you are fortunate enough to attend a service, you will find the standard of music matches the quality of the surroundings. Indeed, the choir from the church provides some of the singers for the chorus in the Passion Play. The fine organ is used for teaching local children and is part of the great emphasis placed on music and drama in local education. Fittingly, all the arts of Oberammergau find expression here. There is also a Protestant (Lutheran) church close to the Passion Play Theatre. This is a more modern style and part of its role in the past has been to offer daily Holy Communion services during the Play season.

In Eugen-Papst Strasse you will find a building which has been provided from the funds of previous plays. This is the **Ammergauer House**, a kind of community centre which includes an outdoor theatre, a concert hall and restaurant, as well as the local Tourist Office. If you would like to see where profits from other plays have been spent, you could pay a visit to the **Wellenberg Recreation Centre**, which is near the cable-car station for the Laber and is open both summer and winter. This really must be one of the most beautiful recreation centres anywhere in the Alps, with a marvellous swimming pool complex. Here you will find three open-air and three indoor pools, two water slides, an adventure pool, large sunbathing areas, saunas, solarium, and a restaurant and bar.

The Ammergauer valley really is an area of very great scenic beauty and since Oberammergau is, as already stated, virtually surrounded by mountains, much of this beauty can be appreciated from below. But if you have the time and inclination then do take to the hills. An after-dinner walk across the river and along King Ludwig Strasse offers a panoramic view and an easy climb to the **Kreuzigungsgruppe**, a 12-metre-high stone monument sculptured in marble and depicting the crucifixion, with the crucified Jesus accompanied by his mother and his closest disciple, John. This was presented by King Ludwig as an expression of his admiration for the people of Oberammergau following his visit to the Play in 1871. Needless to say, this was a

The Kreuzigungsgruppe, a gift from King Ludwig in 1871

special performance after the public performances were finished and attended only by the King and four companions. The Crucifixion Group was inaugurated four years later, on 15 October 1875, to honour the 50th birthday of Ludwig's mother, Marie. The erection of this was not, however, without human cost, for during the process both a master stonemason and a stone-cutter were killed when the specially constructed carriage built to convey the statue of St. John overturned and crushed them. Interestingly enough, it was as a result of the King's visit and by his command that the first photographs of the Play's dramatic scenes and tableaux were taken.

THE PASSION PLAY –
AN INTRODUCTION

The Text

The one used for several decades was basically that of **Alois Daisenberger**, a former priest of the village, for the 1850 performance. The original text, however, seems likely to have been borrowed from other passion plays then in existence, because the tradition of staging the events of Holy Week is believed to be at least 1,000 years old. Moreover, it is probably fair to say that the Oberammergau version has its roots in the medieval mystery plays which were common all over Europe in the Middle Ages. They existed in several countries, including Britain, where the plays at Chester and Coventry are still performed. Plays which told the story of Christ's Passion were a later development and are likely to have grown out of the tradition, as regularly happens today, of reading the accounts of Christ's betrayal, arrest, trial, crucifixion and resurrection as an integral part of the Christian liturgy of Holy Week. From this it was only a small step to dramatise the readings, act out some of the main characters and add music. There is sufficient documentary evidence to prove the existence of passion plays in the 13th and 14th centuries, but there are very few examples of actual texts until the 15th and 16th centuries.

As far as we can be sure, the earliest identifiable Oberammergau text dates to 1662, consisting of 4,902 lines based on a late 15th-century play from Augsburg and a 16th century play from Nuremberg. In 1674, scenes were added from the Weilheim Passion Play, dated to between 1600 and 1615, and this in its turn appears to have had its origins in an earlier 15th/16th-century Passion.

While there were some revisions to the text in 1720 and 1740, a completely new script was written for the 1750 performance by Father Ferdinand Rosner, a Benedictine monk from nearby Ettal monastery. This is often referred to as the *Passio Nova* and consisted of some 8,457 lines of verse using the formal language of the sacred Baroque theatre. The emphasis in this version was on the Devil as the inspirer and instigator of the treatment meted out to Jesus. Though it created stirring theatre it was open to the criticism that it strayed too far from the New Testament narrative. In 1770 the Bavarian government banned all passion plays

The Last Supper

but the persistent protests of the Oberammergauers paid off and the Play was once again allowed in 1780 and 1790. For these performances the text was revised, reduced to 4,809 verses and hell was confined to musical interludes!

Not surprisingly, there was concern that the authorities might return to their banning ways, so in an attempt to head off this possibility, a completely new text was submitted in 1811 by yet another Benedictine monk from Ettal, **Father Othmar Weis**. Out went the Devil and in came the gospels! The aim was to present a drama of the suffering and death of Jesus which was much more in line with the Gospel accounts. Weis also concentrated on the central idea of atonement, removed the allegorical, mythical and legendary elements, and introduced contemporary

theology, prose style and wordy moralising interpretations of the tableaux, along with references to social conflicts. He did, however, keep one dramatic effect from Rosner and that was the special **living tableaux**, eighteen scenes from the Old Testament reflecting the journey of Jesus through the last days of his ministry. The music for this was composed by **Rochus Dedler**, a local teacher and about whom more is said later in this chapter. In 1815 there was a special performance of the Play at the end of the Napoleonic Wars, when there was further extensive revision of the text by Weis and of the music by Dedler. This was also seen as an opportunity to enlarge the crowd scenes, including the 'Entry into Jerusalem.'

For 1850 there were some amendments to the script by Alois Daisenberger, a pupil of Weis and priest of Oberammergau from 1845, who made further revisions at the government's request. Daisenberger gave preference to the Gospel of John and tried to demonstrate the drama of the Passion. By the use of old texts, by warm-heartedness, vivid language and simple symbols, he aimed to 'popularise' the Play, but in the very best sense of the word. Between them, Weis and Daisenberger enabled the Play to emerge from a secular era and once again become the dramatic spiritual force it had been in earlier years. Although there were some subsequent changes over the ensuing decades, whether in the text, the costumes, the staging or the music, the Weis-Daisenberger version was to remain the standard until the major reforms of 2000.

The text, however, was not without its controversial elements. It seemed to present a clear contrast between good and evil, the good being the Christians and the evil the Jews, even though, of course, Jesus, his family and disciples were all Jews. It is highly unlikely that the people of Oberammergau had any intention of producing a Play that was deliberately anti-Semitic. Indeed, anti-semitism as such did not really raise its ugly head until the latter part of the 19th century, long after the Daisenberger text. It is much more likely that the text was consistent with the prevailing theology and popular conceptions at the time in which Weis and Daisenberger lived and wrote. After all, however unpalatable it is now, there was a long tradition of calling Jews 'Christ-killers', going back, for example, to St. John Chrysostom in the 4th century, who spoke of the Cross being ridiculed 'where Christ-killers gather.'

Difficult, too, in the text was the much repeated 'blood curse' of Matthew 27:25, 'his blood be upon us and our children.' The repetition merely served to enforce the prevailing attitude towards the Jews. Nor was the matter helped by the visit of Adolf Hitler to the Play in 1930, accompanied by his propaganda chief, Joseph Goebbels, though, of course, National Socialism had not yet taken control of Germany. The controversy was further compounded in 1934 when Hitler, as Chancellor of Germany, once again attended the Play for its 300th anniversary performances and gave it his approval, writing some eight years later, 'It is vital that the Passion Play be continued at Oberammergau, for never has the menace of Jewry been so convincingly portrayed as in this presentation of what happened in the times of the Romans. There one sees in Pontius Pilate a Roman racially and intellectually so superior, that he stands out like a firm, clean rock in the middle of the whole muck of Jewry.' Not the best advertisement for the Play – to say the least!

Because of World War II there was no Play in 1940 and performances re-commenced in 1950. It was inevitable, after the Nazi treatment of the Jews and all the horrors of the Holocaust, that the question of anti-semitism in the Play should again be raised. It was not until 1965, however, and the Second Vatican Council initiated by Pope John XXIII, that there was the incentive to re-examine the whole issue. The Council decreed that Christians should show a new and positive attitude towards the Jews and that, whether ancient or modern, they bore no collective blame or guilt for Christ's death.

Certain attempts were made between 1969 and 1989 to revise the text in ways which would counter the criticisms, but although some of the worst caricatures in the text were removed from the 1970 Play, yet still there were fierce protests from both American Jewish groups and some Christian ones. One Rabbi described it as 'a nightmare of anti-Jewishness.' An attempt to deal with the situation was made by certain reformers within Oberammergau who suggested ditching the 19th-century Daisenberger text altogether and returning to the older and less passionate Rosner version of 1750. After all, Rosner's allegory-filled verses blamed the Devil rather than the Jews for the Passion of Jesus. Money was raised for a trial production in 1977, which was applauded by the critics, but the villagers, who had the final say about the Play and its text, missed the familiarity of Daisenberger. In the 1978 elections to the Town Council the supporters of Daisenberger won the day and immediately decided that his text would again be used for the 1980 production. There were, however, some changes in an attempt to soften the anti-Jewishness. For example, in the scene when the crowd was shouting for Barabbas to be released, voices were heard calling for Jesus to be set free, and Roman soldiers, too, were portrayed as being vindictive towards him, whereas in the past they had often been presented as standing above the whole furore. But still the 'blood curse' from Matthew's Gospel remained.

Yet change, however slow, was waiting in the wings. Representatives of the American Jewish Committee and the Anti-Defamation League began working with leading Catholic scholars and negotiating with the villagers about changes in the Play, emphasising, for example, the Jewishness of Jesus as well as the role played by the Roman authorities in his crucifixion. Though the whole matter of the 'blood curse' had been particularly divisive, it was retained for 1990.

Eventually, the criticisms of Jews and Christians, both Catholic and Protestant, began to bear fruit and for 2000 a completely new production was commissioned. In collaboration with **Christian Stückl**, the Director, **Otto Huber**, a schoolteacher and the Deputy Director who had been a leading negotiator in the dialogue, undertook the responsibility of creating the new text which involved 60 percent of the original text being re-written. Out went the 'blood curse'; the Jewishness of Jesus and his disciples was strongly emphasised; at the Last Supper a Menorah was prominently displayed and the disciples were shown wearing prayer shawls; Jesus offered a blessing in Hebrew; and the prosecutors in the Council were challenged by several of their own number demanding a fair trial for Jesus. While the preface to the 1990 production argued strongly for the retention of the 'blood curse', the 2000 one declared, 'the Passion Play is in no way meant to find a specific person or group guilty, or even less, to assign collective guilt.' There is even the admission in the same preface, 'that this Passion Play, too, contributed in various ways to preparing the soil which eventually yielded the terrible harvest of the extermination of the Jews. In addition, and significantly, Christians forgot that Jesus was a Jew, like his mother, like Mary of Magdala or all of the apostles, and like the first Christian community.' To assist with all these changes of text, and in particular the matter of how the Jews should be portrayed, a major innovation was the appointment of a Theological Advisor in the person of Professor Dr Ludwig Mödl, a religious historian at Munich University. To be fair to Otto Huber and others who had worked so hard to address the criticisms of anti-semitism, a genuine effort was made to expunge from the Play those elements which in the past caused so much offence.

In preparation for 2010, many hours were spent by the Director, Christian Stückl and Otto Huber, in further adapting the text to both project Jesus' radical message of love to a present-day audience and also to banish any lingering criticisms about anti-Jewishness. To this end both Christian and Jewish advisers provided invaluable assistance. The preface to the 2010 performance included these words: 'It is important for the people of Oberammergau that the Play accurately portray Jewish religious and cultural elements in order to avoid even the possibility of linking the Play with anti-Semitic tendencies, as has so tragically occurred in the past.'

As for 2020, at the time of writing in early 2019, there are only the beginnings of detail about further textual updates. And given the Director's conviction that, 'For the Play to live, it must evolve' then we can only expect changes. The Director has announced that the role of the Teller of the Prologue and the accompanying text have been axed, which will free up more time to project what he describes as 'the positive message of Jesus,' something that he feels (understandably) has been overshadowed by the cruelty and suffering of the Passion. Certainly, it is already anticipated that, as in each new performance, there will be new costumes and tableaux, and given a changing world and changing audience it is equally

The Choir

likely there will be some textual changes as the Play attempts to communicate the meaning of Christ's death and resurrection to a contemporary situation.

The Music

Though there may be less to be written about the music, it does not mean that the musical score is regarded in Oberammergau as any less sacrosanct than the text itself. Far from it! Composed by **Rochus Dedler** (1779–1822), the music has been and remains an integral part of the Play. A production without it is hardly conceivable.

Dedler was born in Oberammergau, the son of a local innkeeper. His musical education began as a chorister at the neighbouring Augustinian monastery of Rottenbuch. It continued in Munich, considered at that time as the best educational establishment specialising in music. Besides having an excellent bass voice, he was regarded as someone with an outstanding musical talent. He returned to Oberammergau in 1802 as a teacher, choirmaster and organist and was to spend the remaining 20 years of his life here, achieving considerable fame, both locally and beyond, primarily as a composer of sacred music. In a comparatively short time he had composed more than one hundred pieces, including some 20 masses and requiems, which are still sung in the parish church.

Unsurprisingly it is his music for the Passion Play by which he is most fondly remembered in the village, even today. Prior to Dedler most of the Play's music

Tableau: The Loss of Paradise

consisted of Gregorian chants and vocal arias, and whether he was influenced in his composition by any of this earlier music is unknown. He wrote different versions for the Plays of 1811, 1815 and 1820, each time to new texts by Othmar Weis. It must be remembered that even for the 1820 Play he was still writing for a production in the cemetery, which inevitably restricted the size of both the chorus and the orchestra. Dedler himself conducted, recited the lengthy prologues to the 24 Old Testament scenes and, in addition, sang the bass part. This was a colossal undertaking for one person and led to a breakdown in his health from which he died two years later.

His score for 1820 reflected the stylistic tradition of the liturgical music of Franz Joseph and Michael Haydn and was, of course, designed to be performed by amateur musicians. It contained solo parts for all four voice ranges in the form of recitatives and arias as well as many choral numbers. The music acts as mediator between the 'living pictures' of the Old Testament and the drama of the Passion, helping to convey the spirit of the drama.

The change of venue in 1830 from the cemetery to a site on the northern edge of the village meant an altogether more large-scale production attended by larger audiences. This in turn necessitated bigger musical resources which therefore required considerable re-writing of the original score. With changes to the text later in the 19th century, some of which involved cuts, the composition had to be further altered. The constant pressure for change continued into the 20th century and this demanded a re-writing of the score for almost every season of the Passion Play. For the 1950 production Dedler's score was greatly enhanced by **Prof. Eugen Papst**, another Oberammergau-born musician, who was a friend and colleague of Richard Strauss. His thoroughgoing adaptation, which among other things added brilliance to the orchestration, led to 40 years of relative musical calm. The unsuccessful attempt in 1977 by some in the village to return to Rosner's text expressed a desire for the Play to be reformed from what had traditionally been handed down. All this was to pave the way for the enormous changes in 2000, both in the text and the music.

Although the text changes required a re-consideration of the music, the original score of Dedler still lay at the heart of the 2000 production from beginning to end. However, the newly written text and the new tableaux from the Old Testament needed new music to be composed. This was the enormous responsibility of **Markus Zwink**, the Music Director who, to achieve what was required, himself composed new music, but in a style that was in harmony with Dedler, and in addition he adapted and revised some of Dedler's own previously unused compositions. Given then that there were further changes to the text and tableaux for 2010, additional music was also composed. There will also be new pieces for 2020, again composed by Markus Zwink.

The Tableaux Vivants and Stage Sets

The Tableaux Vivants or 'living' tableaux are static scenes, motionless pictures, depicting stories from the Old Testament which are staged between scenes of the living Play. For example, the interrogation of Jesus by Annas and Caiphas is preceded by the tableau of Job in misery before his so-called 'comforters', and the scene of Jesus on the way to the Cross is prefaced by the tableau of Abraham demonstrating his complete trust in God as he prepares to sacrifice his only son, Isaac. They serve both to hold the attention while the scenery is being changed, as there are no curtains to be drawn, and also to provide a parallel link with the New Testament narrative. They are accompanied by music and usually by the Chorus or soloists. The actors in the tableaux are entirely motionless, giving the impression of a living scene frozen in time.

These tableaux have been an integral part of the Play since the 18th century when they were introduced as an aid to prayerful meditation, for at that time they were intended to be seen in silence. They are meant also to reveal a basic truth of human experience and divine revelation, and it is through them that successive directors have been able to express their individuality.

The Entry into Jerusalem

From 1930 to 1990 the stage sets were those designed by **Johann Lang**, who produced the Play from 1930 to 1960. Though Christian Stückl was appointed Director for the 1990 Play, at that point he really had to work with Lang's sets, but in 1997, having been commissioned by the Town Council to prepare a new production, he was able to bring in **Stefan Hageneier** to design the sets and costumes. In spite of all the changes to sets, tableaux and costumes in 2000, there were further changes for 2010 and there will definitely be new costumes and tableaux as well as new sets for 2020. The costumes are all created by women from the village. These changes, plus any to parts of the text, are all part of the Director's determination to keep the play alive. He is convinced that each production requires a totally new approach to keep it fresh for a changing audience in a changing world.

The Chronology

Much has been said in this and other chapters about the changes that have taken place in the Play over decades and, indeed, centuries. Yet however much it has changed, the outline of the Play has remained much the same since 1634. Beginning with the Entry into Jerusalem (since the performances of 1815) it takes us through the momentous events of Holy Week – the Last Supper, Gethsemane, the betrayal and arrest, the mocking and scourging, all leading to the final climactic scenes of the Crucifixion, the Resurrection and Exaltation. However much the presentation inevitably changes, the events remain the same and so, too, does the message of the Passion, even though periodically it has to be re-written so as to communicate that message to a contemporary audience.

THE PLAY – ITS ORGANISATION AND TRADITIONS

The **organisation** of the Play is no mean feat, either in terms of the production itself or the managing of nearly 450,000 visitors from 40 different countries during the season. In fact, the overseas visitors make up some 55% of the total number attending the Play. Out of a local population of 5,400 people there are about 2,500 who are involved in the production in one way or another, either on stage or behind it, in the orchestra or chorus, or dealing with scenery, costumes and 'props'.

Since the rest of the population is largely involved in the business of catering for the 4,500 people, plus coach drivers, tour escorts and other staff, who arrive for each

Jesus clears the traders from the temple

performance, coming and going five times a week, it is easy to imagine the colossal impact the Play makes on the community. Then there is the fact that it also creates some problems in carrying on with everyday life, jobs and careers, especially when this disruption happens for only one year in ten. There is only a minute permanent staff retained for the interim years, though the business of tourism does provide many jobs all year round – for most it is a matter of 'business as usual', not only in the years when there is no Play, but also during the Play season itself. It is not unknown for leading actors to have used up all their annual leave and then having to take extra, unpaid time off, to fulfil their roles on stage and at the same time keep their employers happy!

As can be imagined, the handling of visitors is a huge operation in itself. In 2020, for two performances a week, tickets will be sold as part of a package which also includes two nights accommodation with dinner and breakfast, plus lunch on the day of the Play (the day after arrival) and then departure after breakfast on the next

morning. There is the same number of one-night packages available but on different days from the longer stays. Those attending the Play on Fridays, for example, will arrive during the Friday morning, have lunch, see the Play with a dinner break included, and then leave after breakfast on the Saturday morning. Many of the weekend tickets are ear-marked for people who live within easy travelling distance of the village, so on those occasions there will be fewer accommodation packages, but all Saturdays and a few Sundays will have the one- or two-night arrangements. It sounds complicated, but it works!

Because the number of hotels and guest houses in the village is limited, a good deal of the accommodation is provided in private homes. It has long been a tradition for people to open up their houses for visitors to the Play, and for many visitors it is a particular delight to share the home and enjoy the hospitality of a local family. There is strict quality control over the accommodation and food. Since 2010, all rooms are classified and expected to be en-suite, with the banks making special offers to enable householders to improve the standard of their rooms. I remember when I took a group to Oberammergau in 1990 we opted to stay in private homes. In the house where some of the group and I were staying, the daughter of the family that served our breakfast said that she would be appearing on stage during the morning and that we should look out for her, but that she would be back in time to serve our lunch! Similarly, during the afternoon she was on stage again and then came back to serve our dinner, eager to know our reaction to the Play. As you will have guessed, these were in the days when the Play was morning and afternoon. So, you never know, you might be staying with Peter, or Pilate, or Caiaphas or some other prominent member of the cast! But even with the use of private houses, Oberammergau is still not large enough to accommodate everyone, and some will find that they are staying, whether in hotels, guest houses or private homes, in a nearby village such as Unterammergau or Ettal, or a hotel in another resort such as Garmisch or Murnau.

As well as accommodation there is also the question of transport, as most visitors will be travelling to the village by coach from quite some distance away as part of an organised tour. In 2000 it was decided that tourist coaches should be kept out of the village centre, so a system of local shuttle buses was introduced to ferry visitors between the large car and coach parks set up on the edge of the village and the Theatre, and so it has remained ever since. People staying near the centre of the village can, of course, walk quite easily to the Theatre. So transport itself is a vital part of the organisation.

All this coming and going during the Play season gives the impression of a constantly mobile population, for while the population live and work here, an almost equivalent number are either arriving or departing on five days of the week. The only periods of comparative peace and quiet are during the performances themselves, but even then there are constant comings and goings, for many of the cast will have walk-on parts during the bigger scenes and only need to be in the Theatre for small sections of the Play. In between times they can get on with their

The Via Dolorosa: Mary recognises her son

normal lives, running their businesses or homes. Outside the Play season, of course, the village takes on a rather more tranquil air.

Moreover, the staging of the Play itself requires much organisation. As well as the main roles of Jesus, Mary, Peter, Judas, Pontius Pilate and Caiaphas, there will be 120 major and minor speaking roles, as well as soldiers, priests and the people of Jerusalem. In the Palm Sunday scene there can be as many as 500 people on stage. Two players are cast for each of the 18 main parts. Interestingly enough, one of the most coveted roles is that of Judas, who has a major scene and, therefore, the stage all to himself! Previously there were understudies who took minor roles but asking any one person to undertake 100 performances over a period of five months is to impose too great a strain, especially if he or she is employed in business. Also, the selection of two people for the major roles has the advantage of deflecting media attention from the more prominent actors, for example, Jesus and Mary, as considerable effort is made to avoid any aura of stardom being placed on individuals. In the past there have been a limited number of speaking roles for women, but in 2010 a new female character was introduced – Claudia, the wife of Pilate, who appears in person to warn him of her dream. Again in 2010 the Roman soldiers were more prominent in order to portray the political situation between the Romans and the Jews, and part of this was the emphasis on the relation between Caiaphas and Pilate. Nor should the animals be forgotten: the sheep, the doves and, of course, the donkey ridden into Jerusalem by Jesus, as there is much pride in their selection too. In addition, it needs to be remembered that behind the public presentation of the Play is a rigorous schedule of rehearsals which begin in November 2019 and last for a total of eight months, and sometimes there can be three or four rehearsals a week, come rain snow or whatever.

Not surprisingly, given the Play's long history, it is steeped in **traditions**, though some have been gradually eroded over the decades and centuries. To take part a person must have been born in the village or have lived there for 20 years, but if someone from outside the village marries into it then that period is reduced by half. At the end of the Second World War there was an influx of refugees from Eastern Europe, which expanded the population quite significantly. They were assimilated successfully and became eligible to take part in the Play from 1970. The cast is made up of Catholics and Protestants plus several who have no church affiliation, and in 2000 some actors came from the Muslims who live in the village. And for 2020, for the first time ever, the Second Director of the Play will be a Muslim.

Any child who attends a local school can also take part, and there are quite a number of service families in the village from the various NATO countries, as that body has a training school nearby. These facts illustrate what the Play is – a production by a village community where young and old appear together, a nine-week old baby with a 90-year-old veteran.

For the men of the village who want to take part on stage, it means that they must grow their beards and hair because traditionally, on Ash Wednesday the year before the Play, the 'Hair Decree' comes into operation. However, some will later have to shave and cut their hair if, for example, they are chosen to play Roman soldiers, who were always clean shaven. But it is good business for local barbers when, immediately after the final performance of the season, a large number of men from the village are wanting their beards shaved off and their hair cut!

It is the traditions relating to women that have caused the most controversy, especially in recent years. The original position was that no woman could take part who was married or over the age of 35. But for the 1990 Play it was decided, though not without much controversy, that married women would no longer be barred. At the same time the age limit of 35 was also discarded, the result of sex-discrimination legislation following a case in the state court of Bavaria brought by three women from Oberammergau. Prior to these changes it was not unknown for women to put off marriage for many years in the hope of playing Mary or Mary Magdalene.

Up to and including the 2000 Play it had been the inviolable tradition that the performances were spread over the morning and afternoon, beginning at 9.30am and ending around 5.30pm with a three-hour lunch break between the two halves. Nevertheless, for the 2010 production the Director, Christian Stückl, declared that he wanted to spread the performances over the afternoon and evening, beginning at 2.30pm and ending about 10.30pm (timings change by minus one hour from 17th August when the evenings draw in) with a three-hour dinner break. His main reason for suggesting the change was to heighten the drama of the Crucifixion when there could be a more imaginative use of lighting and torchlight. He said that a later performance would 'bring the audience to a different emotional level and improve the quality of the Play.'

As you may be able to imagine, in a village as conservative as Oberammergau, the very thought of this radical change from the norm caused considerable division and heated argument within the village. There were those who argued that it would be unwise to have the person playing Jesus, dressed only in a loin cloth, suspended

The Hair Decree, Ash Wednesday 2019

on the cross in the cold night air for up to half an hour, that children would have to be kept up late, that visitors could get lost trying to find their way back to their accommodation, and that souvenir shops would lose out because visitors would have no time to shop as had previously been the case. Hoteliers complained about the need to provide extra staff late at night to meet the demands of the returning villagers. Others felt it was a much too radical move away from the Play's medieval traditions.

So, the scene was set for a battle between the traditionalists and the progressives, though in essence the conflict boiled down to something much more basic, art versus commerce. Enough signatures were gathered around the village to force a referendum on the issue and this was held on Sunday, 17 June 2007. As can be imagined the debate was fierce right up to the vote. Even the then Mayor came out in support of Stückl by declaring, 'highest priority must be given to the quality of the production, rather than the number of chambermaids we need.' As it turned out the vote went Stückl's way, with the proposed change gaining a majority of the votes. But the Mayor paid the price at the ballot box in the municipal elections a little later on. A centuries-old tradition was therefore set aside for 2010 and the same pattern of afternoon and evening will apply in 2020.

As things worked out, commerce did not lose out to art. It is quite understandable that the village shopkeepers feared for their livelihoods because clearly the number of visitors during the Play season is crucial to their continued well-being. However, for those visitors staying in the village on the two-night arrangement and with the Play not beginning until afternoon, there is free time on the morning to discover something of the village and visit its shops.

The Play is the 'property' of the community of Oberammergau as expressed through its Town Council, and the Council takes all decisions relating to it. Prior to each Play it is supplemented by those appointed as Director, Deputy Director and Musical Director, together with the Catholic priest and the local Lutheran pastor, to form the Passion Play Committee. It is the Council that provides the considerable capital required to finance each production and it is they who provided the necessary funds for the major refurbishment of the Theatre for 2000. A great deal also has to be spent on the infrastructure needed to cope with the influx of visitors: car parks, toilets, drainage and sewerage systems, all of which have to be upgraded and renewed on a continuous programme of works.

Profits from the Play have always been ploughed back into facilities for the community, residents and visitors alike, for example, the Wellenberg Centre and the Ammergauer House, both described on page 18. The village also boasts a Thermal Clinic for the treatment of rheumatic diseases and a Rehabilitation Centre. Education is very important and especially music and drama, into which a great deal of money is poured. Stefan Burkhart, for example, who played Caiaphas in 2000 and Pilate in 2010, first appeared in 1970 when he was only two-and-a-half years old, and Christian Stückl told me that from the age of seven the Play had been very important to him. Whereas in other countries children all have their own special games, whether hide and seek or whatever, in Oberammergau it is not unknown for children to say, 'Let's go play Passion Play,' taking on, no doubt, the particular roles which most appeal to them.

There is some reticence when the question of remuneration for the actors is raised. They are, of course, all amateurs and no one is paid a salary as such. But nowadays it is clearly impractical to expect people to give up such a large proportion of their lives to the Play and possibly suffer loss of income as a result. So players are given an allowance towards compensation for loss of earnings. It is clear that no one makes a fortune from it, so it can be assumed that the arrangement is just about right.

THE PASSION PLAY THEATRE

There has been a theatre on the present site since 1830. However, the first stage for the performance of the Play was erected over the graves of the plague victims and this is how it remained until 1820. During the 17th and 18th centuries the original

simple wooden structure of the stage was equipped with sets and stage mechanics. There was a further overhaul in 1815 designed by the parish priest at the time, Father Nikolaus Umloch. But in 1830 the Play was transferred from the graveyard to a meadow on the northern edge of the village, and this became known as the 'Passion Meadow.' This in turn was to become the site of the present-day theatre. In 1830 the total audiences numbered approximately 13,000, but for the 1840 series this number nearly trebled to 35,000. For 1880 the orchestra pit was deepened so that the musicians could not be seen by the audience, and interestingly enough this was the year in which Thomas Cook of London first began bringing organised tours to the Play.

Ten years later part of the seating area was roofed over, with the rest of the seating area being covered in 1900 by an iron truss structure consisting of six high arches and still existing today. By this time the audiences had risen to 174,000. In 1930 there was a new theatre with an open-air stage designed by Georg Johann Lang, who also directed the 1930 Play, and Raimund Lang who, later as Mayor in the post-World War II days, was responsible for reviving the Play in 1950. In the process of enlarging the auditorium, the original seats in simple rows of benches were replaced by theatre-style seating and this allowed a capacity of 5,200. This was the way it remained till after the 1990 performances. As a result of this enlargement, by 1950 the audiences had risen to 480,000 and this has been more or less the constant number ever since.

However, after the 1990 season it was decided that an extensive renovation of both the interior and the external façade was required. It was felt that the comfort of the auditorium needed to be improved and the stage mechanics modernised. So, in 1997, the villagers were presented with three possible proposals and asked to vote on one of them. Having made their decision, the work began, and within two years the theatre was completely transformed. The seating was renewed; under-floor heating installed; the back-stage area and technical equipment modernised; the cloakrooms extended and toilet facilities improved; the foyer made accessible for wheel-chair users and exhibition areas added; new fire prevention measures for steel and wooden components were taken, and the exterior was transformed. This new theatre provided 4,720 covered seats offering the audience maximum comfort and absolute safety, though for the 2020 performances the seating capacity will be reduced to 4,500 to further enhance the comfort of the auditorium. In addition, all these changes created the opportunity for more extensive use of the theatre for major cultural events outside the Play season.

No-one pretends that the theatre is an architectural masterpiece! It could be likened to a large barn or even an aircraft hangar with its web of iron girders over plain walls. Yet, the rather stark appearance does provide the remarkable acoustical properties which mean that every word spoken on the stage can be heard anywhere in the theatre with the minimum recourse to microphones and loudspeakers. What is more, the design also means that everyone can see as well as hear.

Today's audience is comfortably seated under cover, but in the past the stage has been open to the elements, with the Play continuing whatever the weather

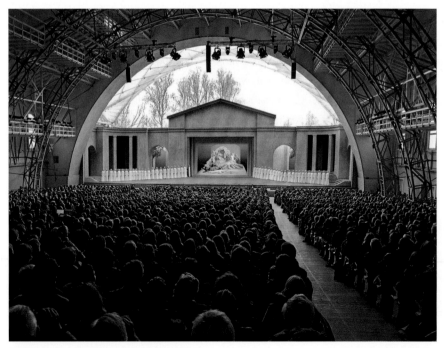

Inside the theatre during a performance

conditions could throw at it. But the setting of the stage with a backdrop of gently rising slopes, the more distant mountains and, hopefully, a few clouds scudding across a clear blue sky, must be one of the most impressively natural for any theatrical performance to be found anywhere. Those occasions when thunder and lightning punctuate the performance may not be comfortable for those on stage, but they can add even more drama to the occasion. So it is that the location provides its own scenery and the stage needs to be embellished only by the simplest of effects. The porticos of Pilate's house on the left and the house of the High Priest on the right are the main elements, with the arches between them representing the entrances to the streets of Jerusalem. The front of the stage becomes the area in front of the Temple, where the main action of the Play takes place.

There is a central stage to the rear, which is covered and has side walls of glass. It is here that the Old Testament tableaux are prepared and presented, as well as some of the scenes of spoken drama. The scene has to be shifted about 40 times during each performance and this requires a considerable amount of technical equipment, including a movable stage and a drop stage, so that scenes can be prepared below, then hoisted up and rolled forward quickly and almost noiselessly as they are needed, for there are no curtains to be drawn to hide this action, as in a normal theatre. There are also electronically driven scene cloths to the central stage, which are wound on to huge steel rollers below.

Since the 2000 changes there has been one significant further improvement and that was the construction of a retractable roof over the stage. Given that in recent years the theatre has been used in non-Play years for a variety of productions, then clearly an open stage became increasingly impractical. Having said that, Christian Stückl tries as far as possible to maintain the tradition of an open stage for the Play itself.

While in previous decades, and indeed centuries, the theatre was reserved exclusively for performances of the Passion Play, it is perhaps hardly surprising that in the 21st century it has been deemed appropriate, both artistically and economically, to move on from that tradition. Since 2005 the theatre has been used in summers for productions of various plays and musical occasions. More recently there has been a performance of Shakespeare's *A Midsummer Night's Dream*, along with operas like Verdi's *Nabucco* and Wagner's *The Flying Dutchman*. So, if you intend to visit Oberammergau during the non-Play summer months, it might be worth checking to see if there is something being performed at the theatre which could appeal to you.

A further possibility in out-of-season years is to take a guided tour of the theatre and its museum, where you can learn much about the origins and history of the Play, as well as discovering something of its influence on the village and its people. You may also have an opportunity to stand on the huge stage and imagine what it is like for amateur performers from the village to play their parts in the great drama of the Play. Also, backstage you will be able to see the rooms where all the costumes are kept, both the more modern ones and those which are extremely old and valuable, some displaying intricate embroidery. There are other rooms, too, where many items of stage equipment, or 'props', are stored. As can be imagined, some of these are very old – the table and stools used in the Last Supper scene, for instance, date back over 200 years. Such a tour lasts about 45 minutes, and from April to October there are tours in English at 11.00am. There are several more options for groups of 10 or more. Be prepared, though, that there may be some restriction on these tours when big events are being staged in the theatre.

Before ending this chapter, mention should be made of the fact that as the Play became more known throughout the world from the late 19th century onwards and as travel to Oberammergau became increasingly possible, so the performances over subsequent decades have been attended by a number of famous people. There have been writers like Hans Christian Anderson, Simone de Beauvoir, Thomas Mann, Jean-Paul Sartre and Rabindranath Tagore; composers such as Franz Liszt, Richard Wagner and Anton Bruckner; as well as the engineers Gustav Eiffel and Henry Ford; members of the Swedish and Spanish royalty, and not forgetting, of course, Ludwig II himself. Other notable visitors have included future Pope Pius XI in 1910, the British Prime Minister, Ramsay MacDonald in 1930, and future US president Dwight D. Eisenhower in 1950.

Pope Benedict XVI visited the Passion Play on two occasions, both prior to becoming Pope. He first came in 1980 as the Archbishop of the Diocese of Munich and Freising, when he also celebrated the opening worship in the Passion Play Theatre. Then, on 23 August 2000, he visited the Play for the second time, on this occasion as Curia Cardinal Joseph Ratzinger, Prefect of the Congregation for the Doctrine of the Faith at the Vatican.

THE PLAY AND ITS PEOPLE

Whatever else may be said about the Play, whether in terms of the wording of the text, the styling of the costumes, the performance of the music or the staging of the drama, basically the Play is about people, those who prepare it and those who perform it.

The Director for 2020 will once again be **Christian Stückl**, who was first appointed as Director for the 1990 Play when he was only 27 years of age, making him the youngest ever. In fact, in 1986, he went to the Mayor and asked if he could direct the Play! Born in the village in 1961, he grew up in the Gasthof Rose, where he met actors and visitors all talking about

Christian Stückl

the Play. He told me that at that stage he would dress up in the costumes and perform lines from the Play, and how he was nicknamed by a former Director as the 'Stage Devil'. This was because he always seemed to be around the Play and its rehearsals, asking the meaning of this sentence and that sentence. Initially he served his apprenticeship as a wood sculptor but having created a group of amateur actors in the village he became assistant director at the prestigious Münchner Kammerspiele in 1987, the same year as he was appointed the Director of the Passion Play. Not unnaturally for 1990, as a younger Director with fresh ideas, he wanted to introduce changes; but with little time for manoeuvre and given that Oberammergau changes slowly, he found himself locked in to the accepted tradition, including the text, though he was able to assign a number of younger actors to leading roles. His style of direction was not without controversy and there were even attempts to dismiss him, but these were narrowly averted. Despite that, however, for 2000 he was commissioned to create a new production about which much has been said elsewhere.

When asked why, as a professional director, he should want to work with the amateurs of Oberammergau, his response is very affirming. Clearly for him, having grown up with the Play and recognising its importance both to the village and far beyond, there is something very special about working with his own people in his home environment. In 1990, for example, he directed both his father and his grandfather who had parts as Judas and Annas respectively. Since becoming Director, he has done much to encourage younger actors to take on leading roles and, as part of the preparation for the Play – he has taken them to Israel so that they might experience something of the setting and background to the Passion story. In the past it was the local committee who had the responsibility for choosing the cast, but increasingly the Director has assumed the responsibility of choice for the major roles.

Since 1990, his career as a professional director has gone from strength to strength. In 1991 he became principal Director of the Münchner Kammerspiele, a post which he held until 1996 when he became a freelance director. He has been a guest director in cities such as Bonn, Frankfurt, Karlsruhe, Hannover and Vienna. More than once he has directed several of the Shakespeare plays, including *A Midsummer Night's Dream* in India. Then, in 2002, he took up the appointment as manager and artistic director of the Munich Volkstheater where he has become noted for his radical productions and encouragement of younger talent. In the same year he was director of *Everyman* at the Salzburg Festival. This was followed in 2004 by his first opportunity to direct an opera, Beethoven's *Fidelio* at the Opera House in Cologne. In the chapter on the Passion Play Theatre, Oberammergau, we have already noted some of his more recent productions there.

We noted previously that as Director of the Passion Play his belief is, 'For the Play to live, it must evolve.' One thing this certainly means is that as long as he remains Director, the Play is unlikely to stand still. And clearly if the Play is both to appeal to future generations and challenge them about the meaning of Christ's death and resurrection, it must do so against the background of a changing world. This in turn means discovering the delicate balancing act of respecting tradition while responding to the present, and I believe that Christian Stückl acknowledges this.

In June 2015, **Abdullah Kenan Karaca** was appointed as the Second Director for the 2020 Play by the Oberammergau Council, an interesting decision in that he is a Muslim, and he will also be one of the two actors playing Nicodemus in the production. Born in Garmisch, he grew up in Oberammergau as the son of Turkish parents and first performed in the 2000 production at the age of 11. In 2009 he joined the Munich Volkstheater as an assistant director, where he worked primarily under Christian Stückl, under whom he also became assistant director at the Salzburg Festival. Then from 2012 to 2015 he studied directing at the University of Music and Theatre in Hamburg and is currently a Director at the Munich Volkstheater.

Abdullah Kenan Karaca

The great significance of music in the Play has already been referred to. Once again, as on three previous occasions, **Markus Zwink** will be the Musical Director, with two second conductors, Eva Kammerer, a teacher from the Gymnasium Olching, and Dr. Christian Wolf of the Richard Strauss Institute in Garmisch. Herr Zwink was born in Oberammergau in 1956, and after completing his education at the Ettal Monastery School, went on to study music at the Mozarteum in Salzburg and the Munich Music Academy. During this time he had the opportunity to be a guest conductor

Markus Zwink

with Nikolaus Harnoncourt. In 1980 he was the bass soloist in the Play and from 1984 to 1997 taught at the Ettal Secondary School, while also being appointed music director of the municipality of Oberammergau in 1985, a post which he has held ever since. In this capacity he runs a number of local choirs, boys, youth and adult, and his wife also runs a girls' choir, all this being part of the village tradition of singing and music.

The Chorus is chosen from the Ammergauer Motettenchor, of which he is the Founder and Director, and the choir of the Catholic church. The Chorus and orchestra for any one performance have about 50 singers and 70 players, and these are drawn from a pool of 120 singers and a similar number of instrumentalists. Many of those singing in 2020 will also have sung on one or more previous occasions, so when it comes to rehearsals a significant number will know the words and music, both of which must be memorised. To sing in the Chorus is much sought-after due to its prominent position on the stage, constantly in front of the audience! There is only one point in the drama at which the singers who are actors appear on stage together and that is in the great scene of the Entry into Jerusalem. However much he may wish that it could be otherwise, tradition makes it very difficult to develop more integration between choir and actors.

In the same way that more than one actor is assigned to each of the major roles, so it is with the soloists, with three or four being chosen for each voice. Sometimes even that may not be enough as there was an occasion in 2000 when all three bass soloists were ill at the same time and Markus Zwink had to take over the bass role. Selection of the choir and orchestra for 2020 took place even earlier than the actors, in 2018. There is a great deal of interest in solo singing and an early start is made with younger singers in assessing their ability to go further. Those who show promise are required to have ten hours training with professional voice teachers from Munich and then they must audition in front of a professional panel.

In the section on The Tableaux Vivants and Stage Sets, something of the crucial work of **Stefan Hageneier** has already been described. Another native of the village and born in 1972, he later became a graduate from the Oberammergau Wood Carving School, and actually took part in the Play as an extra in 1990, and in 2000 shared the role as Teller of the Prologue with Otto Huber, the then second Director. But, of course, his main talents are mainly employed behind the scenes and there will certainly be new tableaux for 2020. These days much of his work is in Munich, collaborating there with Christian Stückl among others, but his skills as a designer have also taken him to New York as well as other major German theatres.

Stefan Hageneier

His reputation has given him the opportunity to work not just nationally but also internationally with a variety of eminent directors in Brussels, Zurich and Vienna.

By now it will have become obvious that there are certain strong family connections with both the village and the Play. A look at some of the names around the village and, in particular, in the cemetery of the Catholic church, is a clear indicator of this. Reference has already been made to Otto Huber, whose family association goes back as far as 1680. His grandfather, Huber Rutz, played Caiaphas three times and Peter in 1950.

Then there is the **Preisinger** family, with Anton now running the Alte Post Hotel, and having played Judas in 2000 and Caiaphas in 2010. His father, Anton, played Pilate in 1980 but his grand-father, Anton was one of the most formidable figures in the village from 1950 when he played Jesus and took the same role again in 1960. He then became Director for the 1970 Play and subsequently took smaller parts in 1980 and 1984, ending in the manner in which he began when at the age of 10 he was an angel and then Lazarus in 1934. And now, Anton Jr. has been selected to play John, perhaps the role most keenly identified with emerging young talent.

Theirs, however, is recent history compared with the **Zwinks**, a family who go back as least as far as 1446. Markus, whom we have already met, is a descendant of Franz Seraph Zwink (1748-1792), the gifted Rococo painter who created most of the earlier frescoes on the houses in the village. In terms of the Play itself, for example, there were three Zwinks in the 1890 production – Rudolf (Jesus), Ottilie (Mary) and Johann (Judas).

Another well-known name is that of **Lang**. They have one of the proudest of family records up to the time of Walter Lang, who played Nicodemus in 1990. The family of Josef Lang settled in Oberammergau in 1736 and it was they who later, in 1886, set up the state wood-carving school. A Lang has played the part of Christ no less than five times – Anton in 1900, 1910 and 1920, who presented a gentler side of Jesus, and Alois in 1930 and 1934, who concentrated more on his heroic nature. However, they lost their 'claim' to the role in 1950 when Anton Preisinger was chosen as Christ, after much local disagreement about who should perform the part.

While much has already been said about Christian Stückl, the Director, in various parts of the book, it is important to acknowledge the **Stückl** family through his father, Peter, and grandfather, Benedikt, both of whom were in the 1990 production when Christian first became Director. In that year, Peter played Judas, having previously been Caiaphas in 1980 and 1984, and Benedikt was Annas, the High Priest, a role which he again undertook in 2000 at the age of 76. He first took part in

1930 and in 1980 was Caiaphas and Herod in 1984. In 2020 Peter will be one of the two actors taking the role of Annas. It is worthy of note that the name of Stückl and that of Zwink were among the original signatories to the Vow in 1633.

But before leaving this chapter we should look at the selecting of the cast and the significance of the occasion when their names are publicly announced. There's a sense in which the Play began on Saturday 20th October 2018. How come? Well, that was the day on which the village both solemnly renewed the original Vow and declared who would be playing whom in 2020 – a most significant day indeed.

The starting point was a morning service at the Catholic church in front of the side altarpiece containing one of the earliest crosses used in the Passion Play.

The children of Oberammergau at the Renewal of the Vow ceremony

A procession, which included the banners and the services of the village and its brass band, paraded through the streets and paused at the Lutheran church for a further act of worship. The crowds then moved on to the Passion Play Theatre for an ecumenical service conducted by the auxiliary Catholic bishop, the priest of the parish church, the Lutheran pastor and the Lutheran regional bishop, an occasion transmitted by Bavarian television. During the service a young girl made the renewal of the Vow on behalf of the village, to which the residents present made it clear that as well as thinking of the liberation of their ancestors from the plague, at the same time they were aware that God would also give life and salvation in 2018 and, indeed, in 2020. Christian Stückl then brought on to the stage all the children

The director reveals the names of the cast members to the scribe

who sing as part of the great opening scene of Palm Sunday, when in the Play itself they, the choir and all who are on the stage greet the entry of Jesus into Jerusalem by singing the wonderfully stirring chorus, 'Hail to you, O David's Son.' But on this Renewal day the audience also had an opportunity to sing with them. A very moving finale.

Then it was on to announcing the much-anticipated names of the main cast. Some 1,830 adult Oberammergau residents applied to participate in the 2020 production, along with more than 500 children to serve as extras. Some male villagers specifically asked to be Roman soldiers as this meant they could shave and cut their hair! This time there were 217 applicants but only 50 places! During previous weeks and months, the Director and his assistant auditioned all registered applicants and cast them in their various roles. In a press conference, Christian Stückl told how the actors' names were presented to the Town Council the previous night. Once again there has been an emphasis on young actors. 'I have taken many young actors in, because we must carry our Passion into the coming generations.' While there was no veto there was, however, some criticism of how the choices were made and how certain people were overlooked, but the process didn't seem to tear people apart! And so, several hundred people gathered at the steps in front of the Theatre in an atmosphere of expectancy and excitement to hear the Director's choices of the leading actors. Whoops of delight erupted from different sections of the crowd as the names, slowly chalked onto two large boards, were revealed as their friends.

So, who would be Jesus? Painstakingly the name began to be chalked up… and once again it would to be Frederik Mayet, who took the role in 2010, and with him, Rochus Rückel, the second youngest Jesus in the history of the Play, very much in keeping with the Director's intention to encourage young talent. Then, what about Mary? Up went the name of the very experienced Andrea Hecht who played the same part in both 2000 and 2010, along with the less experienced Eva Reiser. And for Mary Magdalene? Barbara Schuster and Sophie Schuster – though they are not related. So the process continued until the names of all the major speaking roles were written up on the two boards. This whole event took about 90 minutes, followed by the Director stapling lists of the casting of the minor roles onto nearby boards, for which there was no lesser interest, particularly from the youngsters. As can be imagined, as well as excitement for some there was disappointment for others. It is important to realise that though there is the requirement for two performers for each of the main roles, there is no such thing as an A team and a B team. The performers are completely interchangeable. Lots are cast to see which of the main performers will take part in the premiere, and those not chosen for this automatically fulfil their particular roles in the final performance, which for the cast is as momentous as the premiere itself.

THE LEGACY OF KING LUDWIG II

It may seem strange in a book about Oberammergau to devote a whole chapter to the famous 'mad' King Ludwig II of Bavaria. After all, he has received his fair share of attention over the years through film, television and even two musicals, and the numerous fantasies about his life and death are well documented. In point of fact, in assessing his life and legacy, it is often difficult to distinguish between truth, half-truths and downright fabrication! A colourful but troubled character, he was probably not best suited to the demands of a monarch's life. Yet, whatever

Ludwig II in 1865.

assessment is made of him as a king and a person, the fact remains that he is probably the best-known of the Bavarian kings and in terms of Oberammergau he is regarded as a great benefactor of the village. Here his name is still revered and remembered with great affection, especially on August 24th, the eve of his birthday when the mountain sides are lit up with bonfires and fireworks. What's more, the legacy of his amazing castles is one which can be experienced and enjoyed by visitors to Oberammergau, who can discover them quite easily from here.

Ludwig was born in 1845, the son and heir to Crown Prince Maximilian and Princess Marie of Prussia. Three years later his only brother, Otto, was born. Ludwig's childhood was spent mainly at the **Castle of Hohenschwangau**, which overlooks the village of the same name, and is a few miles from the border town of Füssen, itself the possessor of a fine castle. There had been a castle on this site since the 12th century, with a family of knights being responsible for its construction and maintenance, but from the 16th century onwards it was variously owned and occupied, until by the beginning of the 19th century it had fallen into disrepair. However, in 1832 it was acquired by Ludwig's father, Maximilian, and a year later re-building began and continued until 1837. Restored as a romantic, neo-Gothic castle, it was to become the family's official summer and hunting residence. In the decoration of the castle, Lohengrin, a knight from the illustrious Swan Order and later a leading character in

Castle Neuschwanstein (Anton Brandl, Munich)

Richard Wagner's similarly named opera, features prominently. Swans were used by Maximilian in the castle's decoration as a link to the heraldic symbol of the courts of Schwangau. Wall paintings in other rooms portray the achievements of Charlemagne. During a tour of the castle several reception rooms as well as bedrooms can be seen, and the furnishings include some fine bronzes, carvings and crystals. The grounds consist of fountains, gardens and wonderful views.

Often overlooked in favour of its more famous neighbour, Neuschwanstein, even so it is a castle which merits a visit and combined tickets for both castles can be obtained from the ticket-centre in the village. Hohenschwangau is reached by steep stairs from the village street and from its terraces (for which there is no entry fee) there are excellent views across the valley towards Neuschwanstein.

Not unnaturally, given his surroundings, Ludwig grew up with a deep love of the mountains and their peoples, though in many ways he seems to have developed as a somewhat solitary person, building around himself his own private world. From an early age his artistic flair was apparent, with a devotion to poetry and painting, showing a particular interest in the romantic style. In 1861, at the age of 16, he heard a performance of Richard Wagner's opera *Lohengrin*, the music of which appealed profoundly to his romantic ideals. Three years later, in 1864, when he succeeded to the throne of Bavaria, Ludwig and Wagner met for the first time and for both of them this was to be a significant occasion. It provided Ludwig with a trusted and valued friend, an all-too-rare experience in his life, and for Wagner the unbounded generosity of his King and patron released him from all financial constraints and cares, enabling him to concentrate on developing his great German operas. Here, in Hohenshwangau, Wagner stayed with Ludwig. Here too, Ludwig had his vision of building Neuschwanstein.

Ludwig became king at the age of 18, and his reign can best be described as one of contrasts. On the one hand, he sought to modernise his kingdom, not only through his patronage of the arts, but also by the provision of rather more down-to-earth facilities such as schools, colleges and hospitals. On the other hand, there was the profligacy with which he spent money on a disastrous three-week war with the Prussians and on the lavish construction of the fairy-tale castles. Yet it is with these three magnificent castles at Linderhof, Herrenchiemsee and Neuschwanstein, that Ludwig created his finest legacy for later generations, and though during his life visitors were few and far between, since then countless millions have visited his remarkable creations.

More distant from Oberammergau certainly, and more awkward to visit is

Castle at Herrenchiemsee

Herrenchiemsee, situated on an island in the centre of the huge Chiemsee Lake, Bavaria's largest, between Munich and Salzburg – it can be seen from the A8 autobahn. Access to the castle is possible only by ferry out to the island of Herreninsel. An area of lakes, mountains and unspoiled nature, this is where Ludwig planned his 'New Versailles', a monument to his adoration of Louis XIV. This can be seen from the Great Hall of Mirrors – actually longer than its equivalent in Versailles! The ceiling is painted with 25 tableaux showing the French King at his best.

This is the largest and most lavish of Ludwig's castles. Using the same architect as for Linderhof, George Dollman, it was begun in 1878 and financed by the King's personal fortune and was the last of the castles to be built. The structure was finished in 1885 but only a fraction of the interior rooms were ever completed. Further highlights are the State Staircase, a full-sized copy of the Ambassadors' Staircase in Versailles, and the State Bedroom. Everywhere you look gives the overwhelming appearance of gold and marble. Outside, the spacious gardens are filled with fountains and statues. Yet, for all his personal expenditure on this lavish structure, it is said that Ludwig spent a total of only 16 days here, and those in 1885.

Whichever of the other castles you may choose to visit, **Linderhof** should certainly be regarded as a 'must'. Only about eight miles from Oberammergau, it is on the other side of the mountain range which starts with the Kofel and was inspired by the King's visit to Paris in 1867, as a result of which he became smitten with the idea of building a replica, 'a new Versailles'. This, of course, eventually turned out to be Herrenchiemsee.

Linderhof was the smallest of Ludwig's three castles and the only one he lived to see completed. Though it is much smaller than Versailles, it is quite clear that the palace of Louis XIV was its inspiration with, for example, the staircase at Linderhof being a scaled-down version of the Ambassadors' Staircase in Versailles. Even the Hall of Mirrors was copied from Versailles. As later with Herrenchiemsee, the overall architect was Georg Dollman, who also employed the talents of other designers.

The castle developed from Ludwig's idea of turning his father's tiny hunting lodge at Linderhof into something grander, though initially it was still intended as a private hunting lodge for the king to enjoy. The construction of this miniature masterpiece began in 1874 and was completed in 1878. Ludwig regularly stayed here, and the royal bedroom has an enormous bed, surrounded by magnificent drapes, golden

Linderhof Castle

(Veronika Freudling, Munich)

candelabras and a superb chandelier. One of the reasons that Linderhof is so popular with visitors is because it gives a feeling of being small and intimate, compared with the vastness of Neuschwanstein and the lavish, impersonal character of Herrenchiemsee. There is an atmosphere of domesticity about Linderhof – it looks and feels as if someone could really live here. It became much more like the Trianon at Versailles, Louis XVI's small retreat where he could escape the crowds at the larger palace.

The beautiful terraced gardens cover some 125 acres and combine elements of Baroque style and Italian Renaissance gardens with landscaped sections similar to an English garden. There is a great fountain, lakes and an artificial 'blue grotto', complete with illuminations and gilded shell-like boat. The great cascade of a waterfall is a splendid sight when it is working in the summer, and in the grounds there is also a Moorish Pavilion which was removed from Oberammergau – it was found there in a dilapidated state and was stylishly renovated. A longer walk will bring you to the Hunting Lodge decorated with scenes from Wagnerian operas. Please note that visits within the castle can only be made with a guided group and these are regularly available in English.

The third of Ludwig's castles is the gleaming white **Neuschwanstein**, without doubt the jewel in Ludwig's creative crown. There had been an earlier castle on this site, but Ludwig saw its elevated position as ideal for the realisation of his dreams, a dream world into which he could escape, the poetic world of the Middle Ages. It was originally called 'New Hohenschwangau Castle', but after the King's death it was re-named 'Neuschwanstein', the castle of the swan knight, Lohengrin. This is probably the most photographed castle in Europe, the very epitome of the hackneyed term 'fairy tale', which is clearly why it was chosen to feature in the film *Chitty Chitty Bang Bang*. Given its superb setting, you will not be surprised to learn that from the castle's balcony are the most marvellous views of the area around.

Work started in 1869 with the Gateway building constructed first. Ludwig lived here for a number of years, only moving into the castle proper in 1884. When he died two years later it was still unfinished, with only 14 rooms completed. The interior of the castle is richly panelled and decorated, especially with paintings of the romantic era. The pictures deal with love and guilt, repentance and salvation. Kings and knights, poets and lovers adorn the rooms. There are three main figures – the poet Tannhäuser, the swan knight Lohengrin and his father, the Grail King Parsifal. The picture cycles are based on the medieval legends which Wagner took as the basis for his operas. Not surprisingly, Ludwig dedicated the castle to his great friend.

Indeed, it would not be inappropriate to describe Neuschwanstein as a celebration of Wagner. Of all the rooms, the Singers Hall is the largest and most opulent, where the paintings are by a trio of Munich artists, August Spiess, Ferdinand von Piloty and Christian Jank. The latter, a stage designer, was also responsible for much of the castle's interior design, as also at Herrenchiemsee and Linderhof. It is strange to say, but Ludwig never heard Wagner's music in Neuschwanstein. This only happened some 60 years after the King's death and since then has become a most favoured venue for concerts, sometimes being staged by the light of hundreds of candles.

Access to the castle is from the village of Hohenschwangau. While it is possible to walk up to the castle from the village, a walk of some 30–40 minutes, it is possible to be taken up either by shuttle bus or horse-drawn carriage. The whole visit to Neuschwanstein and the surrounding area really needs a full day. There is splendid walking country both around and within the grounds of both Neuschwanstein and Hohenschwangau. Especially dramatic is the Queen Mary Bridge, which spans a 300-ft gorge near Neuschwanstein, and from here are some of the most breath-taking views of the castle itself. Those with time and energy can make a three-hour walk to the top of the Tegelberg mountain, though there is the easier alternative of a cable-car! You will find plenty of restaurants and other facilities in Hohenschwangau village, which is the base for the visit to one or even both the castles. The **Museum of the Bavarian Kings**, located by Alpsee close to Hohenschwangau castle, is a modern interactive display of some of the Wittelsbach treasures and history.

Close to the village centre are the two lakes which also have romantic associations. The smaller one is known as Swan Lake (Schwansee) and the larger is the Alp Lake (Alpensee). You can walk around both amid majestic mountain scenery.

To describe something of the legacy of King Ludwig II and his strange genius, yet not say something about his mysterious death, would be extremely remiss. Always something of a remote and solitary character, his increasingly bizarre behaviour began to call his sanity into question. More and more he withdrew from his duties as a king and political leader. Though he never used public funds for the building of his castles, the extravagant use of his personal resources meant that by the end of 1885 he was in colossal debt. As can be imagined this caused considerable embarrassment for the Bavarian government and so it was decided to remove him from office by declaring him officially insane.

The certification of Ludwig's insanity was provided in early June 1886 by Dr. Bernhard von Gudden and three colleagues, based on evidence which was no doubt deliberately slanted against the king. What's more, they did not even examine the patient on whose mental state they were to pronounce with such authority. While there were others who regarded the oddity of his behaviour merely as symptomatic of an eccentric character, nonetheless those in authority concluded his madness was incurable and that he was no longer capable of exercising the powers that had been entrusted to him. On June 12, 1886 he was arrested and taken to Berg Castle on the shores of Lake Starnberg. On the evening of the next day, June 13, Ludwig invited von Gudden to accompany him on a walk through the grounds of the castle and later that same evening their drowned bodies were found floating in the lake. As to the precise circumstances surrounding their deaths, no one knows and we never will. One thing is clear – at the age of 40 the 'Dream King' was dead!

Visitor Information

Linderhof Palace & Neuschwanstein

(with Hohenschwangau and Museum of the Bavarian Kings):

Open daily   April – October 15: 9 am – 6 pm;

October 16 – March: 10 am – 4.30 pm (4 pm Neuschwanstein).

Closed January 1, Shrove Tuesday (Linderhof), December 24/25/31.

Linderhof Park buildings closed October 16 – April 14.

The grotto is closed at time of writing, until further notice.

Herrenchiemsee New Palace:

Open daily   March 31 – October 27: 9 am – 6 pm;

Rest of the year: 9.40 am – 4.15 pm.

The King Ludwig Museum has similar hours.

To visit all the palaces in this chapter, a combination ticket of €26 is available. Individual prices vary depending how much you want to see and what season of the year you visit. Full details about admission and how to obtain tickets can be found by visiting www.schloesser.bayern.de and selecting the relevant property.

For Neuschwanstein if you are not with a tour group, tickets should be purchased at the ticket centre in Hohenschwangau, at Alpenstrasse 12, Tel. 08362 930830 and can be reserved for a specified timed visit up to two days in advance (surcharge): www.hohenschwangau.de (includes map).

However, once at the centre there is more information, including the times of tours in English on an electronic board. There are many options, including arrival at the castles by horse-drawn carriage.

VISITS IN THE SURROUNDING AREA

Clearly how much of the local area you will be able to discover in addition to Oberammergau itself will depend on the length of your stay. Those visiting the Play as part of an organised tour may find that the options are somewhat limited, but those on a longer visit will hopefully find time to explore some of the possibilities outlined in this chapter.

The Monastery at Ettal

In a narrow valley around three miles from Oberammergau is the village of Ettal, originally located on the important trade route between Italy and Augsburg. Today it is dominated by the imposing edifice of its monastery, founded in 1330 by an earlier Ludwig who brought back from Italy the white marble Madonna, believed to be a miracle-working statue, which still has pride of place on the altar. Built as a Gothic monastery it had two abbeys, one for men and the other for women, as well as having a community of knights attached to it, and in due course various residents of the community were to become significantly associated with the Passion Play, particularly with refining and re-writing the text. Nowadays it is still a living monastery and parish church, home to approximately 50 monks.

Though it suffered damage during the Reformation at the hands of the troops of Maurice of Saxony, it did at least survive the troubles of the Thirty Years War. In 1744 the monastery, its church and a library of about 30,000 books were largely destroyed by fire, though the precious Madonna was preserved. Re-built as a splendid example of southern Bavarian Baroque style, the monastery was later dissolved in 1803 during the time of the secularisation of church property in Bavaria but was subsequently re-founded as a Benedictine monastery in 1900. The interior of this impressive church is elaborately decorated in white and gold, a fine example of Rococo adornment. The ceiling of the great rotunda is painted with some 400 figures representing St. Benedict and his monastic order, and in the centre hangs a huge chandelier.

The monastery also has a brewery and a distillery which produces a certain well-

Ettal Monastery

known liqueur! In addition there is a bookshop, an art publishing business and even an hotel. A school was founded here in 1709 and this began its educational tradition. These days the school boasts a choir with a high reputation in the locality.

The Church at Wies

Down a lonely country road through forests, some 16 miles from Oberammergau, off the road from Rottenbuch to Steingaden, lies a farm, a meadow, a church and very little else. Standing almost alone, this important church is a place of pilgrimage for Catholics the world over. It is also one of the richest examples of Rococo decoration to be found anywhere in Europe.

Its reputation is built on the legend of the Flagellated Saviour, a statue created by the monks of Steingaden in 1730 to be paraded in the Good Friday procession. However, some years later in 1734 the monks decided that the statue was much too realistic and intense and so was put to one side. Maria Lory, the devout wife of a local farmer, rescued the statue and took it to a farm where it became an object of veneration. Then on one day in 1738 she had a vision of the dilapidated statue shedding real tears. When this became public knowledge there was a rush to see it.

The church at Wies

In 1740 a small chapel was built to house the Flagellated Saviour, but soon became too small to cope with the large influx of visitors who wanted to venerate the statue. So, between 1745 and 1754 the present great church was built, designed by Dominikus Zimmermann, who spent the last 11 years of his life in a nearby dwelling to be near his masterpiece. He was assisted in the project by his brother, Johann Baptist. Though the church was secularised at the beginning of the 19th century, protests from farmers saved this jewel of Rococo design and architecture from being demolished,

While the outside is strikingly simple, the inside is strikingly elaborate. Oval in shape, the interior is adorned with gilded stucco, wood carvings and vividly coloured frescoes, which contrast with the white-washed walls. It has been described as 'exuberant, colourful and joyful.' The quality of the white marble and the gilded decoration, together with the fine carving, impressive paintings and frescoes, all combine to produce a marvellously light effect, aided by the natural lighting through the windows. The church was added to the UNESCO World Heritage List in 1983 and underwent a massive restoration between 1985 and 1991. If at all possible, Wies should not be missed.

Garmisch-Partenkirchen

Some 15 miles from Oberammergau these twin towns, separated by a railway line, have become a byword for winter sports and as a climatic health spa. Settlers first appeared in the area around 2000 BC, and later the Romans established Partanum, which later became Partenkirchen, as a staging post on the military road between Brenner and Augsburg. Originally two towns, each with their own history, they were forced by Hitler to combine in 1935 in readiness for the 1936 Winter Olympics and over the decades since have developed as Germany's best and most famous ski resort. Traditionally, there is a ski-jumping contest held each New Year's Day and in 2011 the Alpine World Ski Championships were held here.

The area is dominated by the **Zugspitze**, at 2,962 metres the country's highest mountain, and in the summer this can be ascended by **mountain railway** from the town centre. With mountains all around and Alpine resorts like Lermoos and Seefeld just a short drive away, Garmisch-Partenkirchen makes a good centre for touring the area. It is an attractive town and an excellent shopping centre, with elegant boutiques, art galleries and antique shops. The old part of the town has narrow streets and features wrought-iron signs. This is an especially good place for walkers as there are a variety of lifts and cable-cars quite close to the town. The composer **Richard Strauss** lived here from 1908 until his death in 1949 and each June he is honoured in the town with a 'Richard Strauss Festival.'

The Zugspitze (2,962 metres) overlooks the town of Garmish-Partenkirchen

Munich

Many visitors to Bavaria in general and Oberammergau in particular, whether for the Play or not, will land at Munich Airport, and if time allows it is well worth spending a day or two in this vibrant capital of Bavaria. 1158 is usually given as its foundation date, with 1175 being the year in which it was granted city status. After Berlin it is Germany's second most popular destination and provides something for everyone – culture, high tech, spacious parks and squares, architecture, beer gardens and, of course, shopping!

Munich was the seat of the Wittelsbach family from 1180–1918. The family included Maximilian, who was the first King of Bavaria (from 1808), and his son, Maximilian II, who made Munich one of the great cities of Europe. His progeny, of course, included our friend, Ludwig II, he of the famous castles. The complex of great buildings known as the **Residenz** reflects the splendour of the family, who lived here from 1385 to 1918. Here, as well as the **Palace of the Wittelsbachs**, is the grandiose **National Theatre**, home to the Bavarian State Opera, the **Treasury** and several other museums.

Nearby is the world-famous Glockenspiel Carillon at the **'new' Town Hall**, one

The Munich Rathaus and Marienplatz from Peterskirche

The Residenz: The Ancestral Gallery (Toni Schneider, Lindau)

of Munich's most famous buildings and erected from 1867 to 1909 in Gothic style. Its main façade is 100 metres in length and decorated with very elaborate stone work. The 85-metre tower of the Carillon is one of the most distinctive features of the skyline and attracts the crowds at 11am each day for a 15-minute display. Do not miss the splendid late-15th-century Gothic **Frauenkirche** (the Cathedral of Our Lady), the interior of which is adorned with works of art spanning five centuries, nor **St. Peter's Church**, the oldest parish church in Munich. This was originally built in the 11th century as a Romanesque Basilica but was later destroyed in the great fire of 1327. It was then rebuilt in 1379–86 in Gothic style, but during the 17th century the interior was re-modelled in a very ornate Baroque style. If you have the energy to walk up to the top, and it is a long climb, you will be rewarded with wonderful views across the city. All this is in a very compact area which is easily walked. With its grand avenues and spacious squares, which recall the glories of Bavaria's monarchy, the old town is a pleasure to visit and stroll around.

Further away there are numerous other museums and galleries, not to mention the parks, the largest of which is called the **English Garden**. The world-famous **Alte Pinakothek Gallery** contains Munich's main display of old European Masters,

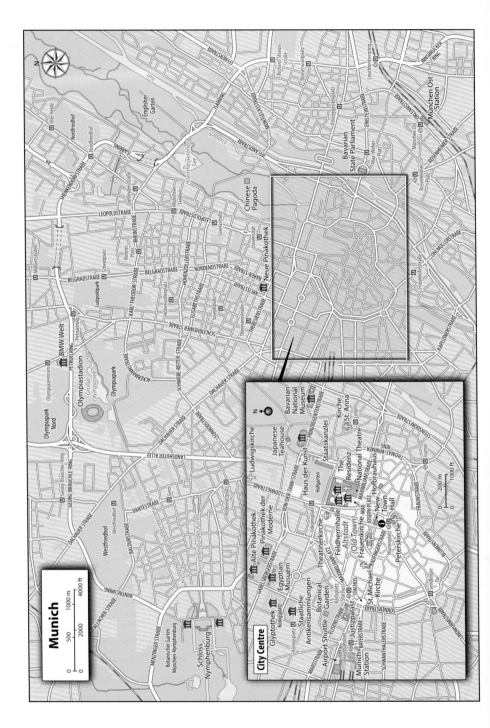

mainly collected or commissioned by the Wittelsbachs between the 14th and the 18th centuries. On the edge of the city is the **Nymphenburg Palace**, created in the 17th century as the royal family's summer residence. Set in a huge park with lovely gardens it today houses a superb art collection.

There are also the **stadia** built for the 1972 Olympics, and the great halls dedicated to Munich's most famous product – beer. The annual **Oktoberfest**, actually held in September, consists of a three-week frolic of eating and drinking, and attracts people from all over the world.

Innsbruck and the Tyrol

Holidays which include the Passion Play will often also include some time spent in the Austrian Tyrol, most of which is within an easy day's drive from Oberammergau. The same, of course, remains true for non-Play visitors – if staying in Oberammergau

then Innsbruck can easily be visited from there and vice versa. Anyhow, wherever you are staying in this region, a visit to the Capital of the federal state of the Tyrol, Innsbruck, is a must, for this fine city is wonderfully situated in the Inn valley with, seemingly, a sheer wall of mountains at the end of almost every street.

The broad avenue, Maria Theresien Strasse, forms its main shopping street, running from the great **Triumphal Arch**, past the **Column of St Anne**, to the entrance of the old city, with its arcaded shops, finely made wrought-iron signs and great stone houses with walls so thick that city defences

Innsbruck City Tower   (Mario Webhofer)

69

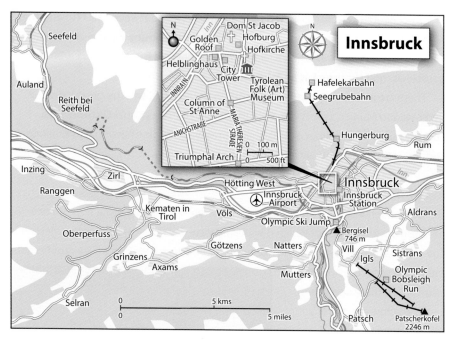

were unnecessary. Inside the old city is the famous Golden Roof covered with more than 2,600 gilded copper tiles, a gallery constructed for the Emperor Maximilian in 1500 to serve as a royal box from which to watch the tournaments and dancing in the square below. Opposite is the **Helblinghaus**, originally Gothic from the 15th century but later covered in 1730 with such magnificent Rococo ornamentation that it became known as the Wedding Cake. The **City Tower** in the same square provides a fine view from the top, and at the riverside entrance to the old town stands a 14th century inn, the **Ottoburg**, with a statue to the Tyrolean Freedom Fighters outside it. Across the road from that is another old inn (16th century), the **Golden Adler**, which had associations with Goethe and Mozart.

Innsbruck was one of the centres from which the Habsburgs ruled a great chunk of Europe and the Royal Palace, the **Hofburg**, was first built around 1460 in late Gothic style and then rebuilt 1754–1773 in Baroque style by Empress Maria Theresa, mother of Marie Antoinette. It has a splendid interior and across from it is the remarkable **Hofkirche**, the Court Church, with enormous bronze statues of the real and imaginary ancestors with whom Maximilian I hoped to be buried but wasn't. Next to that is the very interesting **Tyrolean Folk Museum**, with an outstanding display of lounges, furniture, costumes, farming tools, masks and nativity scenes from the alpine regions.

Great views of Innsbruck and its surroundings can be enjoyed climbing any of the surrounding mountain ranges, but from the hill of **Bergisel** (end of tram line 1), as well as admiring the views you can also inspect the Olympic Ski Jump, a reminder that Innsbruck is an internationally renowned winter sports centre and hosted the Winter Olympics in both 1964 and 1976. The original **ski jump** was built in 1926 and re-designed for the 1964 Olympics, but by the end of the 20th century it no longer met with requirements. A magnificent new one was opened in September 2002 and this striking landmark of Innsbruck is well worth a visit. As well as providing a variety of sports facilities, there are public spaces including a café, as well as a viewing platform. If you don't fancy the steps up there is a funicular to the top. Also in this area is the lovely **Basilica of Wilten**, another example of extravagant Rococo design, probably the finest in the Tyrol.

At the other end of tramline 1, by the river, is the **funicular** to the **Hungerburg**, a small village on a plateau above the city. You can go higher still from here by cable-car to **Seegrube** and the mountain-top at **Hafelekar** (2,334m). The panoramic view includes all of the surrounding mountains, which rise to nearly 4,000 metres, across Innsbruck to resorts such as Seefeld, and to the great Europa Bridge, which leads to the Brenner Pass and Italy. Straight ahead across the valley is the 'sun

The view from Seegrube   (Kathrein Verena)

terrace' plateau below the **Patscherkofel** Mountain (2,246m), surmounted by a radar tower, on the slopes of which the Olympic downhill races have been run. On this sun terrace are the resort villages such as Vill, Igls and Telfes. The cable-car from Igls takes you to the top and to the Olympic bobsleigh run, as well as some excellent walks and stupendous views. From the start of the beautiful **Stubai Valley** can be seen one of the most scenic rides, whether by car, bus or tram from Innsbruck. This is but one of the numerous excursions along the valleys which spread out from Innsbruck. The route from this area towards Garmisch and Oberammergau takes you over the **Fernpass**, one of the most scenic drives imaginable.

At the beginning of this section I mentioned that many groups visiting Oberammergau, whether for the Play or not, may spend some time in the Tyrol as the holiday part of their tour, Innsbruck being a possibility in the scenic Inn Valley. Not far from Innsbruck is **Seefeld**, once a farming village but now a major alpine resort. Set on a south-facing plateau it has become one of the most popular Tyrolean tourist destinations, attracting skiers in the winter and walkers in the summer. Many of the walks in the area are very gentle and not requiring much in the way of hiking up and down mountains! In the town is the tiny **church of Seekirchl**, well worth a visit, and so, too, is the larger **church of St. Oswald**, rich in

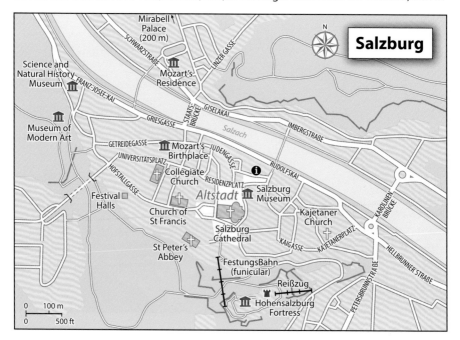

72

A view of Salzburg   (Breitegger Günter)

history and the venue for concerts by visiting choirs during the summer.

Further afield, for example, in the Western Tyrol, you may find a group staying in any one of several Alpine villages and these will have **Salzburg** as their star attraction. Set among mountains and lakes it was the backdrop to *The Sound of Music* and the birthplace of Mozart. Visit the 11th century **Hohensalzburg Fortress**, from which there are wonderful panoramic views of the city and the opportunity to take a step backwards into the Middle Ages. If you are feeling energetic you can go up on foot but if not, there is always the **funicular**! There is also the opulent 17th century **Mirabell Palace** with its wonderful gardens, as well as the 17th century **Salzburg Cathedral**, with its mighty dome and twin towers. But perhaps supremely, Salzburg is known as the birthplace of Wolfgang Amadeus Mozart, Salzburg's most famous son, and every year thousands make a pilgrimage here to pay homage to their great idol. The **Mozart Birthplace** and **Mozart Residence** are both museums that will take you back to the 18th century. But whatever else you do or don't do in Salzburg, do take time to stroll around the Altstadt (Old Town) which is the historic centre of the city. A UNESCO World Cultural Heritage Site, it has a most wonderful collection of medieval and Baroque buildings. And don't forget its busy shops, whether for clothing, leather or whatever else takes your fancy!

Wherever you may spend the 'holiday part' of the tour, whether in one of the many delightful areas in the Austrian Tyrol or elsewhere, you can be sure that your visit to the Play will be the highlight of your journey, a memory that will last.

THE ROMANTIC ROAD FROM ROTHENBURG TO SCHONGAU
Andrew Houseley

The idea of the *Romantischestrasse* as a tourist route emerged in postwar West Germany as motor coach touring was picking up from where it had to leave off in the late 1930s. It seemed sensible to promote and link some of Europe's best preserved medieval walled towns and iconic neoclassical castles, on an old north-south trade route that opens up into some of Europe's most beautiful scenery. Some of the first tourists to take advantage of the route were American servicemen stationed in the new Federal Republic, and it remains to this day an essential feature of the itineraries of many a Stateside tour operator and independent traveller. The Romantic Road has a choice of starting points, but the most common are either Würzburg or Rothenburg ob der Tauber – or it can be done in reverse perhaps from Füssen.

We are going to concentrate on Rothenburg to begin with, however, it should be mentioned in passing that **Würzburg**, as the sixth largest city in Bavaria, has a rebuilt historic centre and is noted for the enormous UNESCO-listed 18th century **Residenz** and the **Marienberg Fortress** – homes of the Prince-Bishops who ruled from the 12th century until the dissolution of the Holy Roman Empire. The ecclesiastical states of Germany were secularized, the city becoming part of Bavaria by 1815. The **Cathedral** is dedicated to the Irish St Kilian who was martyred here, while his relics are in the **Neumünster** basilica. We are also in what is regarded as the region that produces Germany's best wine, Franconia, its vineyards on the steep slopes of the River Main and the Spessart hills.

Rothenburg ob der Tauber
The 12th century castle built by the Stauffer dynasty that began the town was destroyed by an earthquake, only the gardens and a chapel remain, however, despite a turbulent history there is plenty to delight and intrigue. In the 13th century, Rothenburg was granted privileges by King Rudolf of Habsburg and became one of the most important cities of the Holy Roman Empire. A Jewish community had already established itself but was all but wiped out in the

persecutions of 1298 that affected several cities. Equally less welcome was the Nazis' lionizing of Rothenburg as the perfect German town.

As with much of this old trade route, the 17th century Thirty Years War put paid to Rothenburg's prosperity. By this time the city had become a Lutheran stronghold, but in 1631, shortly after Protestant King Carl Gustav-Adolf of Sweden left here, the Catholic League commander, Johann Tserclaes, Count of Tilly, wanted to garrison his 40,000 troops. The population decided to resist and took to the defensive walls which were breached when the gunpowder tower exploded. Tilly demanded the execution of the burghers, however he was entertained with the area's wine served in an enormous 3 ¼ litre tankard. Tilly announced that he would spare the councillors and their town from destruction, if one of them could down the entire contents in a single draught. Up stepped Mayor Georg Nusch, who completed the challenge, much to Tilly's amazement. The **Meistertrunk** (master draught) story is re-enacted in a town pageant, and on the hour in the gable of the city councillors' tavern – **Ratsherrntrinkstube** – when either side of the clock two windows open, one showing the animated figure of Nusch raising the tankard and the other, Tilly nodding in appreciation. Nevertheless, over the next 20 years the city was frequently occupied and besieged, its population oppressed, ravaged and impoverished. In 1802 it lost its independence, annexed to Bavaria.

Apart from the historic tavern, there are several other attractions of the market square **Marktplatz**. The **Town Hall** – Rathaus – is Part Gothic and part Renaissance, its many features include the entrance arcade, the magnificent

The 'Meat and Dance House' by St George's fountain

Imperial Hall, and the tower gallery which affords good views of the town. The **inner courtyard** features archways that used to house shops, and now display historical scenes from the Thirty Years War, with dungeons below. **St George's fountain** is the most notable of several that survive; it nestles between two steep half-timbered gables, one of which is known as the **Meat and Dance House**, because there were butchers' shops under the arches and a hall for festivities upstairs. Behind the square is the large Gothic **church of St Jakob** the German name for St James, as the pilgrimage route to Santiago de Compostela

Plönlein

used to pass through. It has its own pilgrim's shrine, a piece of rock crystal said to have been brought from Golgotha, and containing drops of Christ's blood. It is embedded in the gold cross on the Holy Blood altarpiece, featuring superbly carved figures and tableaux by local master Tilman Riemenschneider, the centerpiece a depiction of the Last Supper. The main altarpiece is another treasure, featuring paintings of the Twelve Apostles on the predella and allegories from the life of St James on panels by Friedrich Herlin from Nördlingen. Back outside, passing through an archway underneath the church brings us to the **Imperial City Museum**. Set in a former convent, artefacts relating to the history of the city include the original Meistertrunk tankard, and rooms include the old kitchen, while the cloister contains the Rothenburg Passion, 12 15th century paintings. Returning to Klingengasse brings us to the **defensive walls** and the **Klingen Tower**, which served the dual purpose of a water tower. Integral to the defences is **St Wolfgang's church** from where the casemates can be reached below the altar and the gate tower via a spiral staircase above.

We can either continue below the walls, left, working our way to the **Castle Gate and gardens**, the nearby **Franciscan church** and noble **houses** back round to Marktplatz, or retrace back to the centre for the most iconic scene of Rothenburg. From Marktplatz head down Schmeidegasse, pass the Renaissance **Master Builder's House** with its statues of the seven virtues and seven vices. Perhaps visit one of the traditional bakers' shops for some sumptuous fruit or walnut cake, or a Rothenburg speciality, *schneebälle* named

In Rothenburg, Dinkelsbühl and Nördlingen the tradition of the nightwatchman is preserved, in which a patrol of the walls and alleyways is carried out, accompanied by the cry "All is well" or something more elaborate according to which town you are in. Tours are available at each location: enquire locally.

for the icing sugar sprinkling over rounded crunchy shortcrust pastry. Now we are at the medieval crossroads of **Plönlein** with the **Siebers Tower** straight ahead and the tower of the **Kobozell Gate** and its customs house leading down the adjoining street, with a half-timbered house in between. This is one of the scenes in the Walt Disney film *Pinnochio* (1940); and then the town appeared in *The Wonderful World of the Brothers Grimm* (1962), *Chitty Chitty Bang Bang* (1968) and *Harry Potter and the Deathly Hallows* (2010 & 2011). The largest **Spital Bastion** is on through Siebers Tower and is part of an historic complex that includes a hospital and the town barn. Doubling back, up along the fortifications, the **Rödertor** is a small complex of towers, guard rooms and customs houses with bridges connecting the inner gate and outer wall. From here, we have another very attractive walk back to Marktplatz. The **Markus Tower** and the **White Tower** further around mark the original walls before the town's expansion. Last but not least the **Medieval Museum of Crime** (Burggasse) displays instruments of torture and also humiliation, including masks of disgrace for gossiping women and men.

South to Augsburg

The Baroque castle on a rock at the spa town of **Schillingsfürst** is visible from the road, while **Feuchtwangen** is another former Free Imperial town. The next really well preserved medieval walled town of note is **Dinkelsbühl**. At the crossroads of two trade routes and situated in the valley of the river Wörnitz, the town is thought to date back to the 6th century, and became a Free Imperial city, making its name in cloth and weaving. Through one of the **gates** and into the centre, a beautiful collection of half-timbered houses around the **Weinmarkt** front the mighty **St**

Dinkelsbühl

George's Minster. The interior stonework, including the tall windows and fan vaulting, is what marks this out as one of the finest examples of late Gothic church architecture in Germany.

Nördlingen lies in the fertile Ries basin, the surrounding hills forming the

Nördlingen and the Ries hills from the Daniel

crater of what scientists believe to be the result of an asteroid strike millions of years ago. Again the fortifications encircling the town are intact and you can walk all the way round its 11 towers and five gates. Allow plenty of time and reserves of energy to climb the 365 steps to the top of **The Daniel**, the tower of **St George's church**. The church is noted for its Baroque altarpiece depicting the Crucifixion and its ornate organ housing. The **Rathaus** features an external stone staircase with fluted columns. A documentation of the Ries crater is one of three **museums** in the town.

The **castle** and small town of **Harburg** is our next stop 23km further south. The quaint town on bank of the Wörnitz is dominated by the castle complex on the hill above. The Staufian castle passed into the hands of the Counts of Oettingen in 1295, where it has remained ever since, developing into one of Germany's best preserved castle complexes, and nowadays run by a non-profit making family trust. Once inside the courtyard, the Fürstenbau wing houses a **museum**, with some carvings by Tilman Riemenschneider among the treasures.

When we come to **Donauwörth** we arrive at the confluence of the Wörnitz and the Danube – making it an important river port in times past. Whilst only one length of the walls and a substantial gate survive, the town is noted for having one of the most attractive streets in Germany, the **Reichs-strasse** (Empire Road) which follows the trade route of the Holy Roman Empire from Nuremberg to Augsburg and on towards Italy. Today, the buildings are painted in pastel shades and photo opportunities are usually punctuated by frequent traffic. At the bottom of the street is the **Rathaus** with its stepped gable, while at the top, past the Gothic **church of Our Holy Lady** and the town **well**, is the **Fuggerhaus**, a Renaissance style residence of the famous banking family from Augsburg.

Augsburg

The city's illustrious history began in 15 BC when the on the orders of Caesar Augustus, his step-son Tiberius and the general Drusus established *Augusta Vindelicorum* as a camp and trading post where the rivers Lech and Wertach converged. It became the capital of the province of *Raetia* and key to the road to Rome, the *Via Claudia Augusta*. In 1276 it was granted the status of a Free Imperial City which only accelerated its prosperity while at the same time this led to frequent tension with the Prince-Bishops of Augsburg from whom the status gave its inhabitants independence. The two merchant and banking **patrician families**, the Fuggers and the Welsers, vied with each other for wealth and influence, propelling Augsburg to the status of one of the world's banking capitals and the construction of wide boulevards, elaborate fountains and magnificent buildings. They lent money to the royal houses of Europe, marrying their princesses and gaining control of overseas territories, Germanic towns and castles in return. Both remained Catholic at a time when the city became such a focal point of the schism of the Church. In 1634–35 Augsburg and its Swedish garrison was laid siege by the Catholic forces, with the population much reduced

Jakob Fugger, by Albrecht Dürer.

by starvation and disease. Augsburg has given many illustrious sons and daughters to Germany, including the painters Hans Holbein the Elder and Younger, composer Leopold Mozart (father of Wolfgang Amadeus), playwright Bertolt Brecht, engineers Rudolf Diesel and Willi Messerschmidt, and also Wolf Blitzer of CNN. Today at nearly 300,000 it is Bavaria's third largest city and a leading industrial centre, particularly in automotive, aerospace and ICT.

Martin Luther had criticized **Jakob Fugger 'the Rich'** (1459–1525) for the sale of indulgences and his pressurizing Pope Leo X to end the prohibition of the levying of interest. It was one such loan from Fugger that resulted in the construction of St Peter's Basilica in Rome. However, he is credited with establishing the first social housing complex in the world, the **Fuggerei** which can be visited today in the east of the city centre. The criticism of papal indulgences for the absolution of apparently in some cases, any sin, was worked into several of Luther's **Ninety-five Theses** of 1517. Luther mistakenly thought that the pope would agree with him, but instead he was put on trial. The papal legate, **Cardinal Cajetan** summoned Luther to Augsburg where he stayed at the Carmelite monastery – now the Lutheran **church of St Anne**, and so began the hearing on October 12th (continuing on the 14th) 1518 which took place in the **Fuggerhaus** in the then *Weinmarkt*, now Maximilianstrasse. Cajetan demanded that the scholarly Augustinian monk recant and return to the fold, but Luther insisted on discussing his Theses. The hearings degenerated into a loud heated argument with neither side backing down. Fearing imminent imprisonment, Luther with the help of friends, escaped at night from the city through a small gate near the chapel of St Gallus; at the replacement church an inset plaque marks the spot with the cry of Da Hinab! or 'down there!' He was excommunicated and his struggle continued. The church of St Anne also contains the **Luther Steps Museum** in which a display with audio dramatically recreates the interrogation; the sumptuous Fugger family **chapel** remains. The city gave its name to the **Augsburg Confession** – the essential confession of faith of the Lutheran church – that was agreed at the Imperial Diet of Augsburg in 1530 in front of the Emperor Charles V. Luther the outcast was not present at what by this time was a considerable triumph. The city was again at the centre of things in 1555 as the **Peace of Augsburg** attempted to reconcile the Catholic and Protestant faiths, though unsurprisingly, tensions and persecutions continued as the Wittelsbach dukes aimed to consolidate Bavaria as Catholic.

Martin Luther, by Lucas Cranach the Elder

Display at the Luther Steps Museum

Most tours of the city centre begin at the impressive **Town Hall**. Built in the renaissance style by local master builder Elias Holl between 1615 and 1624, it replaced a Gothic structure as a symbol of the city's wealth and reach. Inside, the main attraction is the magnificent gilded and painted wooden ceiling in the

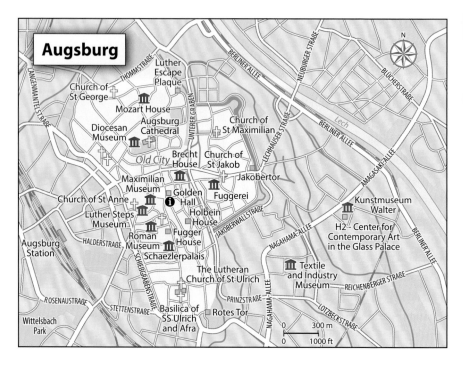

Goldener Saal (Golden Hall). Heavily damaged by World War Two bombing, it was not initially restored to its original style and splendour, only being so for the city's second millennium in 1985. Next to the Rathaus is the 70-metre high tower, the **Perlachturm**. Originally a medieval watchtower, Holl added the dome to complement the Rathaus and a carillon of bells plays a merry tune at certain hours of the day. The vast Rathausplatz has the ornate **Augustusbrunnen Fountain** at its top corner. To the south is Maximilianstrasse the showpiece street. Past the Fuggerhaus and the **Hercules Fountain**. The **Schaezlerpalais** (1770) has a fine Rococo façade. Originally built for a wealthy silver merchant and named after his son-in-law, it now houses three art collections connected by its magnificent **ballroom**. The German Baroque collection at the front of the building is very extensive but not top quality, while the Haberstock collection includes a few of the works the art dealer to the Nazis kept for himself. Through into the former 16th century St Catherine's convent, the **Staatsgalerei** houses the paintings of Roman basilicas by Holbein the Elder, with the picture of Jakob Fugger by Dürer. Try not to miss the formal **garden**.

At the end of Maximilianstrasse we see what in fact are two churches, one adjacent to the other. The smaller Protestant **church of St Ulrich** was originally the chapter hall

Rathausplatz, Augsburg

of the monastery that was given to Lutherans in 1710, and contains some fine detail. The larger **Basilica of St Ulrich & St Afra** is the former monastery church and contains the tombs of the two patron saints of the city in the **crypt**. St Afra was martyred on

Ceiling panels in the Goldener Saal

this spot, thought to be the site of a Roman cemetery, in 304. Ulrich, a former Bishop of Augsburg, was the first saint to be canonized by the pope himself (993).

North of *Rathausplatz*, five minutes' walk, we find the city's **Cathedral** (Dom). There are at least three architectural styles on display, but outside, Romanesque-Gothic is most easy to discern. The stained glass of the five prophets is the oldest series of its type in existence, and the altarpiece paintings are by Holbein the Elder. The crypt, containing the tombs of former bishops, is another standout feature. Near the west entrance is the **Diocesan Museum** displaying the original bronze door.

There are several other museums, including the **Maximilian Museum** (Fuggerplatz 1) displaying sculptures and examples of goldsmithing. The **Roman Museum** (Zeugplatz 4) concentrates on finds from the city's time as a provincial capital. The **Mozart House** (Frauentorstrasse 30) is quite evocative despite the fact that the family had moved before the prodigy son was born; he returned to give several recitals in the city. The historic centre slopes east towards the river and first to the system of parallel **lech canals** that were the centre of early industry and artisans' houses, utilizing water power. Remains of the city fortifications including two gate **towers** (east and south) can be seen.

Towards the Alps

The expansive nearby town of **Friedberg** where Elvis Presley was stationed has a pretty square (*Marienplatz*) with Rococo town hall and fountain. East of *Marienplatz* is the pilgrimage **church Herrgottsruh** (The Peace of God) with fine choir, frescoes and stuccowork. The **Wittelsbacher castle** and museum (north) is the other main attraction.

Schmalzturm (or Schönerturm) in Landsberg.

Landsberg am Lech was founded in the 12th century by Bavarian ruler Henry the Lion to protect the salt trade route. The town was plundered during the Thirty Years War. Hitler was imprisoned here in 1923, from where he wrote *Mein Kampf*. The concentration camp outside the town became a displaced-persons centre after liberation in 1945. The old town by the river's weir retains much of its medieval charm. The architect of the church at Wies (see Visits in the Surrounding Area, pages 63–64) Dominikus Zimmermann, lived here and produced the stuccoed **Town Hall** and the **Johanneskirche** with its fine altarpiece. **Bayertor** – the white decorated Munich gate tower – can be climbed for a panoramic view and to see the workings of its clock.

Rathaus by Dominikus Zimmermann

Schongau is 28Km further south along the Lech. Another town that guarded the salt route, its walls, towers and gates are very well preserved. Leading off the wide town square with its steep gabled **Ballenhaus** – a former warehouse converted to the Town Hall – the **church of the Assumption** is another by Zimmermann, while the **Basilica of St Michael** in adjoining **Altenstadt** provides contrastingly sober Romanesque decoration. On the opposite side of the river, **Peiting** provides access to the first sizable Alpine peak, **Hoher Peissenberg** (998m) and its **pilgrimage church** of the Assumption and connecting **chapel**, another Rococo delight. We are now in the charming Bavarian district of Pfaffenwinkel. Besides the most admired Rococo church at Wies, the twin-towered **Abbey at Steingaden** is also worth a visit if time allows, as its ceilings combine paintings with white barrel vaults. So too, the former Abbey at Rottenbuch! It might well be a question of how much Rococo decoration you can stand in one day. Continuing south on the Romantic Road leads us to the castles and the chapter, The Legacy of King Ludwig II.

SOME PRACTICAL DETAILS

Getting There and Around

Oberammergau is situated some 100 km (60 miles) south of Munich and can be reached by **car** from the European motorway system; the A95/E533 to Garmisch-Partenkirchen. Prior to this road the alternatives are the A8/E52 via Stuttgart and Augsburg, or the A9/E45 via Nuremberg and Ingolstadt – either will take you through Munich. As an alternative, consider joining the A7 after Würzburg to Nesselwang and following the B roads east. If driving direct from Munich Airport (located to the northeast of the city) take the A92 – A9 – A95 and estimate at least 1½ hours. From the channel ferry ports the distance is some 1,000 km with about 10 hours actual driving time plus hold-ups. The last leg of the journey, on the B23 having left the motorway, is very scenic, rising up from Oberau to the Ammergau valley, through Ettal.

By Air, the major international airport is at Munich www.munich-airport.com National carriers include: Aer Lingus; Air Canada; American; British Airways; Delta; Emirates; Lufthansa (with by far the widest choice of destinations); Singapore; South African; and United (five departure airports at time of writing). Easyjet fly from several UK airports. For more European budget flights, Memmingen www.allgaeu-airport.com has opened up in the last decade; it is situated northwest of Oberammergau (A96 – B17 – B23) and is a pleasant 1½ hours drive with limited public transport connections.

Oberammergau can be reached on the European **railway** network, including the white painted Inter City Express (ICE) trains operated by *Deutsche Bahn*. There is a subway and rail station at Munich airport, connecting to the city's main *Hauptbahnhof* from which there is an hourly service to Oberammergau with a change at Murnau (journey time one hour 50 minutes). There is one extra departure from Oberammergau after the end of each Passion Play. This is a very scenic journey on a line built in 1900, and claimed to be one of the most beautiful in Germany.

The wider area is served by the **RVO Bus network**. It is part of DB, German railways – look out for the red-painted buses. After each Play there will be a departure to Garmisch-Partenkirchen at 11pm. See www.bahn.de for bus and train options. For **coach** travel see https://www.flixbus.co.uk/coach/oberammergau.

Seeing the Passion Play

As we have noted, nearly all tickets for the Passion Play are sold as part of a package, with a one or two-night stay in the village or surrounding area included with breakfast and meals. These packages can be bought independently or will be part of a very wide range of escorted tours. If you want to travel independently, you will need to book your Passion Play arrangement or ticket-only on the www.passionsspiele-oberammergau.de website or call the dedicated line +49 (0) 8822 83 59 330 Monday–Friday. Early booking is strongly advised, and that never fails to catch out thousands of people, who habitually make their travel arrangements a year in advance or less. But at time of writing, mid 2019, there are still some tickets available for every performance except the Premiere. Do not purchase overpriced tickets from commercial booking sites. For those whose only hope of seeing the play is to arrive on spec, then tickets that have been returned can be available at a kiosk by the Theatre – arrive when it opens in the morning. An introductory lecture was provided in 2010 in the Passion Play Theatre on the morning of performances.

Information

There are two distinct points of contact: for the Passion Play, and for tourism. The Ammergau Alpen Tourism Region www.ammergauer-alpen.de runs the main **Tourist Office** which is in a corner of the Ammergauer House complex, on the river side of it rather than the village side:

Eugen-Papst-Strasse 9a
82487 Oberammergau, Germany
Tel. +49 8822 922740
info@ammergau-alpen.de

There are smaller tourist offices in Bad Bayersoien, Ettal, Saulgrub, and Unterammergau.

For the **Passion Play**, the main office is at the Rathaus (Town Hall) which since the last Passion Play relocated to the historic Pilatus House www.passionsspiele-oberammergau.de. There is no public desk, but on the website you will find extensive information on how to book, performance dates and times, the history of the Play, and more. On Facebook search for @passionplayoberammergau and on YouTube search Passionsspiele Oberammergau. Address:

Eigenbetrieb Oberammergau Kultur
Ludwig-Thoma-Strasse 10

82487 Oberammergau, Germany
Tel. +49 8822 949880 Fax +49 8822 9498856
E-mail: info@passionsspiele-oberammergau.de
Expect it to change again after 2020.

For information on tours of the Oberammergau Museum and the Passion Play theatre see www.oberammergaumuseum.de. To keep in touch with other performances at the Theatre see www.passionstheater.de. For those who want to relax on any free time in the village, the swimming pool complex has its own website: www.wellenberg-oberammergau.de. **Wi-fi hotspots** are at the Theatre, the Ammergauer House, and the garden of the Pilatus House.

The extensive collection of Bavarian State palaces, gardens and lakes is managed by www.schloesser.bayern.de and the State's tourist board provides further touring planning at www.bavaria.by. For those venturing into Austria, www.tyrol.com and www.salzburg.info can, alongside this book, be your starting points.

There is a complimentary **Visitor's Card** in the Ammergauer Alpen region, issued at your hotel, which allows discounts on various attractions and some free bus travel. The more extensive **KönigsCard** is provided by some guest houses and holiday apartments, and is especially useful if you are planning excursions in the wider area, and like to use cable-cars, rental bikes or free admission tickets. Neither card can be purchased independently.

Church Services and Ecumenical Centre

No firm decision for 2020 has been made at time of writing. However, in recent Passion Play seasons, a programme of support for visitors has operated, with the Lutheran church next to the Theatre as its hub. Advice and information has been available in English. At the 2010 play, an ecumenical Hymnbook was produced for special services, with music and English translation from the German. At the parish church, mass in German is available to visitors at all times, and during the Passion Play, confession or spiritual counseling is available with some English. In 2010 the parish also hosted a meditative light installation showing important figures in the play's history and allowed viewings of the plague death register; expect something similar this time. Of course, if you are part of a group who wish to worship together, many hotels will provide a room to do so; you could find an open space perhaps by the river, maybe the open-air theatre at the Ammergauer House is available, or you can enquire about the aforementioned services. If in Munich, a list of church services

in English together with a wealth of other information is available here:
www.toytowngermany.com/wiki/English-speaking_church_services_in_Munich

Shopping
As already noted, hand-carved figures are the number one souvenir from
Oberammergau. What follows on, from toys and dolls, to cuckoo clocks to a branch of
the famous German Christmas store, to beer steins, hats and full Bavarian costume, and
to all manner of other crafts – all are here. During the Passion Play the official souvenir
book is of the art book 'coffee table' variety with stunning pictures from the latest
performance; some visitors might consider it too large and heavy for their luggage, in
which case it is available to order in the UK and North America. Other official Passion
Play merchandise includes recordings of the music, hats, t-shirts and pens. For everyday
requirements, there are quality stores in the village selling clothing and electrical items;
also those useful German drug store chains. There are three banks, each with an ATM;
the smaller neighbouring towns and large villages all have at least one each.

Emergencies
For Fire and Ambulance and Police **dial 112** from any phone – works across Europe.
For Police you can instead dial 110 in Germany; the police station in Oberammergau
is at Feldiglgasse 17. If you are taken ill, get assistance from your hotel or hosts, who
can call a doctor, or for less serious complaints go to a pharmacy for advice.
For genuine emergencies: the US Consulate in Munich, dial 089 2888-0; the
British Consulate-General is in Munich with a pan-Germany emergency number,
089 211090; for Irish citizens, 030 220720; Australian citizens can call their
government, +61 2 6261 3305, and there is a Consulate-General in Frankfurt; New
Zealand citizens should first dial 30 206 210 for the Berlin embassy. The Canadian
Consulate in Munich general number is 089 2199570, email: sos@international.gc.ca

Time Zone
All of Germany and Austria are on Central European time: BST +1; EST +6: AEST -8.

Electricity
The European 2-pin/prong power plug is used on 230V 50 Hz AC. Modern low
wattage items (laptops 100W max, tablets, phones, cameras, shavers) should present
no problems in charging if you bring one or two suitable standard travel adaptors.

AND FINALLY...

If, as stated at the beginning, the Play is Oberammergau and Oberammergau is the Play, what does the future hold as the community and its prized possession progress through the 21st century and hopefully beyond? What is the future of the Play and, indeed, how far into that future can the original vow 'till the end of time' be maintained?

I suppose the short answer is that no one knows, especially given the current apparent decline in interest in religion in the West. It can only be assumed that over the centuries since the first performance in 1634, this question about the Play's future viability will have been aired on several occasions. When you consider the various political turmoils over the years, the wars not only in Europe but involving the world-wide community and, of course, that period at the end of the 18th century when passion plays were banned in Bavaria, though Oberammergau managed to stand out against the ban, there must surely have been those who wondered, privately if not publicly, what the future held. Yet here is the village now, in 2019, preparing for the 43rd production of the Play in honour of that original vow, or 'the Wow' as some pronounce it in English.

Maybe one of the reasons that

Ecce Homo (Behold the Man)

the Play has survived so long is that over the centuries the people of Oberammergau have realised, sometimes reluctantly I suspect, that tradition does not have to stand still. I mention again Christian Stückl's dictum, 'If the Play is to survive, it must evolve.' Tradition which is static dies, but tradition which is understood as a living experience can have a future. To maintain the tradition of the pledge, the Play has had to change, not only in the present but in the past. For example, the texts of Rosner in the 18th century and of Weis and Daisenberger in the 19th illustrate the village coming to terms with changing situations. As we saw, the re-writing of the text by Father Othmar Weis for the 1811 production, the 1810 having been banned, was an attempt to head off any future prohibition by the authorities. Now obviously in the past change has not always come easily, nor without some acrimonious debates between traditionalists and modernisers. After all, the village has tended to be extremely conservative about the Play and changes have often come slowly, yet they have happened – even though sometimes later rather than sooner!

But prior to the 2000 production it was plainly recognised that with the dawn of a new century, that was an appropriate moment at which to make wholesale changes, not simply for the sake of it, nor just to answer the justifiable criticisms of the Anti-Defamation League and others about the perceived anti-semitism of the text. Rather, it was an opportunity to present the Play in such a way that the meaning of Christ's suffering, death and resurrection could speak to and challenge 21st century audiences. For the Oberammergauers, the Play has never just been about theatre, however important the manner of presenting the drama of the Passion may have been. It has been an expression of communal faith, an act of worship, a mission undertaken by the village in response to the Vow, and a mission on behalf of the world-wide community. And to be realistic, at a practical level it is also an extremely important feature of the local economy. These, then, are the underlying motives which have moved the Play forward from decade to decade and century to century, and which I believe will continue to project it forward into an unknown future.

Maybe the more recent attempts to encourage younger actors into the major roles, including 2020, will be seen as a vitally important way of entrusting the meaning as well as the tradition of the Vow to future generations. Certainly, at the moment, there seems to be no let-up among people in the village.

THE CAST

As we have noted the Cast were selected in October 2018. The following details are correct as of that time.

Jesus

Frederik Mayet
Age 38. Artistic Director for Munich Volkstheater and Press Officer for the 2020 Passion Play. Played Jesus in 2010 and John in 2000.

Rochus Rückel
Age 22. Aerospace Engineering Student. Was an extra in 2010.

Mary

Andrea Hecht
Age 47. Retail Sales clerk and Wood Sculptor. Her third consecutive appearance in this role, she has also played Mary Magdalene in 1990 and previously a Chorus member.

Eva-Maria Reiser
Age 34. Flight Attendant. Played Mary Magdalene in 2010. She is also a musician and was an orchestra member (violin) in 2000.

Mary Magdalene

Barbara Schuster (nee Dobner)
Age 31. Recruiter. Played the same role in 2010.

Sophie Schuster
Age 23. University Student / Bank Clerk. An Extra in 2010.

Caiaphas

Andreas Richter
Age 42. Psychologist. Played Jesus in 2010 and Archelaus in 2000.

Maximilian Stöger
Age 30. Forest Ranger. Played Peter in 2010.

Judas

Martin Schuster
Age 29. Political Scientist. Played John in 2010, a Servant at the Last Supper in 2000.

Cengiz Görür
Age 18. Student. An Extra in 2010.

Peter

Martin Güntner
Age 31. Production Equipment Mechanic.
Played Ezekiel in 2010, previously an Extra.

Benedikt Geisenhof
Age 29. Geologist. Played John in 2010. An
Extra in 2000.

John

Anton Preisinger Jr.
Age 20. Hotel Management Student. An
Extra in 2010.

Christoph Stöger
Age 21. Law Student. Was a Servant at the
Last Supper in 2010.

Pilate

Anton Preisinger
Age 50. Hotelier. Previous roles include
Caiaphas and Judas.

Carsten Lück
Age 49. Technical Manager, Workshop
Manager. Played Judas in 2010 and 2000.

Annas

Peter Stückl
Age 76. Restauranteur. Played this role in 2010; Previous roles include Judas and Caiaphas (twice each). Present since 1950.

Walter Fischer
Age 77. Retired Senior Educator. Has participated in every Play since 1950. Also Joseph of Arimathea in 2010 and Pilate in 2000.

Joseph of Arimathea

Christian Bierling
Age 53. Special effects Technician. Pilate in 2010.

Anton Burkhart
Age 48. Forest Ranger. Played Caiaphas in 2010, and Jesus in 2000.

Nicodemus

Jonas Konsek
Age 32. Project Planner. Played Peter in 2010.

Abdullah Karaca
Age 29. Theatre Director and Second Director to the Passion Play. An Extra in 2000.

Simon of Bethany

Matthias Müller
Age 49. Horticultural Engineer. Archelaus in 2010 having twice played Nathaniel, Priest.

Hubert Schmid
Age 55. Forest Ranger. This is his seventh Passion Play.

Herod

Simon Marschalek
Age 25. Business Student. His third Passion Play.

Maximilian Laubert
Age 26. Medical Technology Student. Also his third Play.

Nathaniel

Kilian Clauss
Age 21. Mechatronics technician apprentice

Sebastian Dörfler
Age 27. Retail Sales Clerk.

Archelaus

Fischer, Simon
Age 36. Carpenter. Played Nathanael in 2010 and John in 2000.

Tobias Eich
Age 41. Carpenter. Played the same role in 2010.

Gamaliel

Benedikt Fischer
Age 35. Restauranteur. His fifth Passion Play.

Walter Rutz
Age 54. Is the Director of the Passion Play operating company of the Town Council. His sixth Passion Play.

Ezekiel

Dietrich Schneider
Age 29. Dramaturgy and Press Assistant

Julius Iven
Age 20. Law Student

FOLLOWING THE ACTION – A SYNOPSIS OF THE PLAY

This is a brief Synopsis of the Play as it unfolds on stage, which should enable the visitor to follow the action as it happens – it is of course all spoken in German. There is a Text Book which gives a word by word text in English, and this will probably be given to visitors who are on a package on arrival at the theatre or when they check in to their hotel – but it is by no means easy to follow the action on stage and the text in the book at the same time.

Although we have taken into account the Director's stated intention to remove the Prologue to each Act and with it the Teller of the Prologue role, there will doubtless be further changes made in the run-up to the Premiere, and these may indeed include substitute Tableaux, changes to the sequence of some scenes and new passages of action.

We think however, that the "plot" is so well known that members of the audience will have no difficulty in following the action.

Prelude: Jesus is proclaimed Saviour (Soloists and chorus)

Tableau: The Loss of Paradise (Adam and Eve)

Musical Selection: by Choir and orchestra

Part One of the Passion

Act I – Jerusalem

Jesus enters Jerusalem on a donkey, accompanied by a jubilant crowd.

Act II – Jesus with the Friends in Bethany

Tableau: The Israelites – guided by Moses – are saved at the Red Sea.

The disciples tell of the miracles they have witnessed Jesus perform and Peter identifies him as the Messiah, the Son of the living God.

Jesus and his friends, including Lazarus, Magdalene, Martha, Thaddeus and Andrew are visiting Simon of Cyrene at his home. Judas expects Jesus to be proclaimed King of Israel and liberate them from the Romans. The others agree; Jesus disagrees but they do not understand.

Magdalene anoints Jesus with a very expensive oil, and Judas objects to the waste of money which could have been better spent on charity. Jesus defends Magdalene and predicts his death at the hands of the Romans. He describes his dying both as defeat and victory. Magdalene understands and responds with a passage from the Song of Songs: "Strong as death is love".

Mary, along with Joseph, Simon, Jacob, Judas and other relatives accuse him of irresponsibility because he has not settled down and started a family. Jesus tells them they will weep and lament, but the world will rejoice. Judas says that he is tired of believing and hoping.

Act III – Expulsion of the Temple Merchants – Caiaphas encounters Pilate – Judas and the High Council

Tableau: The Ten Commandments and the Dance around the Golden Calf.

Scene 1: Jesus drives the money changers from the Temple. Several merchants protest. The crowd shout Hosanna and proclaim Jesus as Messiah (a term which is interpreted as a challenge against Rome). The crowd start to sing a traditional Jewish pilgrimage psalm, praising God. After the violence of the expulsion, Jesus sets the scrolls in their correct place amid silence. Ezechiel, Nathaniel and Archelaus urge Caiaphas to have Jesus arrested for leading the people astray and undermining the foundation of their faith. Caiaphas counsels patience because Jesus has too many followers and the Romans may take bloodthirsty reprisals.

Scene 2: Caiaphas, the High Priest given powers by Pilate over law and order in the city, tries to reassure the Governor that there is no plot of revolt and that Jesus is not a threat. Pilate believes otherwise and reminds Caiaphas that the land and people will be plunged if there is rebellion against Rome.

Scene 3: The High Council discuss what to do. They consider imprisoning Jesus but Caiaphas concludes he must die. Several Priests are horrified but Annas and Nathaniel support Caiaphas.

Scene 4: The High Council discuss how to arrest Jesus, then Judas enters and makes himself known as one of the Nazarene's disciples. He expresses doubts. Caiaphas reassures Judas that they only want to question Jesus, not kill him, and cajoles him to lead them to him. Judas will be paid 30 pieces of silver.

Act IV – Jesus celebrates with his disciples the Last Supper

Tableau: The Paschal meal before the Exodus from Egypt. We are invited to compare Moses's meal with that which the Lord will celebrate with his disciples. A chorus of Israelites calls for liberation from Egyptian servitude.

Jesus gives the traditional Passover blessing and tells the disciples that he came from God and is about to return to God, but will come again to the world. He washes their feet and together they pray "Our Father". He shares the bread and wine with the disciples in a scene which is commemorated by Christians everywhere in the Sacrament of the Holy Communion.

Judas leaves after Jesus accuses him of planning his betrayal, and the others prepare to follow Jesus to the Mount of Olives.

Act V – Jesus at the Mount of Olives (The Garden of Gethsemane)

Tableau: Betrayal of Amasa by Job at the rock of Gibeon.

Scene 1: Judas and his fellow conspirators are approaching. Judas tells them how he will identify Jesus with a kiss.

Judas's kiss

Tableau: The calling of Moses before the burning bush. Jesus is seen kneeling in the olive grove; weeping and screaming he offers himself to the Father.

Scene 2: In the olive grove, Jesus and the disciples discuss the events to come. There is confusion and misunderstanding. Jesus tells the disciples that they will take offence at him, and Peter that he will deny him. He also predicts that they will be persecuted for his sake and be filled with the Spirit of Truth when needed.

Jesus prays alone while the disciples are asleep. He pleads for mercy and yet is ready to accept God's will. He is almost overcome with the weight of humanity's sins. An Angel appears and asks Jesus to be pierced and crushed by humanity's sins in order that salvation might reach to the ends of the earth; Jesus accepts the charge.

Judas and the rabble arrive along with some of the priests. Judas hurries up to Jesus and kisses him. Peter strikes Malchus's ear with his sword, and Jesus heals the wound, after commanding Peter to put his sword away. He then gives himself up to be arrested.

Musical Selection: The chorus sings of the coming battle of agony and we are reminded in a duet that the shackles on the hands of Jesus are ransom for our freedom.

Interval

Part Two of the Passion

Act VI – Jesus before Annas and the High Council

Tableau: The Prophet Daniel in the Lion's Den. Sentenced to death because he has honoured his God.

Tableau: The mocking of Job. Job in misery, taunted by family and friends, bearing the torment patiently.

Scene 1: At Annas's house, some councillors and Judas arrive. Judas learns confirmation that Jesus is to die and says this was not his intention. Annas reassures Judas he has done his duty. Councillors and Temple guards arrive with Jesus. Annas interrogates Jesus asking what he has been teaching. Jesus replies that Annas knows the answer because he has been teaching in the temple and one of the men slaps him in the face for impudence. Annas accuses Jesus of dissenting from the renowned teachers and that he claims to be greater than Abraham.

Scene 2: Before Caiaphas, the High Council decide they must put Jesus on trial. Jesus is charged with a number of religious violations including blasphemy. Several witnesses testify to the accuracy of the charges. Jesus does not defend himself. When asked if he is the Messiah Jesus answers in the affirmative. Several councillors say Jesus must die. Nicodemus and Gamaliel object to the decision, and Joseph of Arimathea agrees pointing out that Jesus is not accused of a crime punishable by death. Since only the Romans have the right to order and conduct executions, Jesus will next be taken to the Governor's office.

Act VII – Jesus is mocked – Peter denies Jesus – The despair of Judas

Tableau: The despair of Cain who has killed his brother (Judas appears).

Scene 1: Judas wanders aimlessly. He wants to return the blood money in the hope that Jesus will be released but realises that this is a foolish hope.

Scene 2: Several members of the temple guard and women are warming themselves by a fire when Peter and John arrive and are invited to join them. Jesus arrives and the guards decide to entertain themselves by manhandling and mocking their prisoner, calling him a king and spitting at him. When Peter is accused of being one of the Nazarene's disciples, he vigorously denies even knowing Jesus and breaks away and runs off.

Scene 3: Peter deeply regrets his cowardly denial of his friend and teacher and promises that nothing will ever separate him from Jesus again.

Scene 4: At the High Council, Judas rushes in and demands the release of Jesus. He accuses them of condemning an innocent man and throws down the blood money. The councillors dismiss his pleas and leave Judas to despair, planning to hang himself.

Act VIII – Jesus before Pilate and Herod

Tableau: Moses is expelled by the Pharaoh.

Scene 1: Members of the High Council hope that Pilate will support their decision. Pilate treats them with arrogant disdain, angry at being awakened and at their presumption that Caesar's Governor should serve as a blind tool for carrying out their decisions. When told that Jesus called himself the Son of God he considers the entire proceeding superstitious nonsense. Caiaphas and Annas then accuse Jesus of crimes against the Emperor. They use Jesus' claim to be the Messiah as proof, since both Jews and Romans understand the term to point to a military leader who will liberate the Jews from the Romans. Pilate dismisses the councillors and interrogates Jesus alone with guards. Jesus tells Pilate that he only has his power because it is granted from above.

Jesus before Pilate

Scene 2: Herod, the King of Galilee, happens to be in Jerusalem for the festival. When he meets Pilate, Herod desires to meet Jesus with Pilate only too willing to hand him over, despite protests from Caiaphas. Herod tries to get Jesus to entertain him, by interpreting a dream, or causing darkness to fall, or walking without touching the ground, or turning a stick into a snake. When Jesus does not perform, Herod calls him a fool. Herod has no intention of getting involved in Jesus' trial even at Pilate's invitation, and after mockingly dressing him in a royal cloak, advises Pilate to release him.

Scene 3: Pilate again interrogates Jesus, striking with a whip and asks, is he King of the Jews? Jesus answers, "You say it". Jesus is scourged and mocked by the Roman guards. His tormentors dress him in the king's mantle, put the crown of thorns on his head, and hand him a stick for a sceptre. They throw themselves down before

Jesus, jeering, "we salute you, great and mighty King of the Jews!" Pilate offers to release a prisoner for the Passover festival, an ancient custom, and suggests the people decide which prisoner, so that they can have their king if they want. Caiaphas protests, knowing that it will be the end of his power, and sends the priests out to the city to gather an enthusiastic crowd.

Narrator and chorus

Act IX – Jesus condemned by Pilate

Tableau: Joseph is celebrated as Saviour and King of Egypt.

Nicodemus and John discuss what might have happened to Jesus. The crowd arrives, different groups are screaming their support for the release of Barabbas and the release of Jesus. Members of the High Council shout out the crimes of which Jesus has been accused. Nicodemus tries in vain to reason with Caiaphas and the others, who accuse him of being followed by prostitutes and tax collectors, even pagans. The mob screams that Jesus should pay for his blasphemy on the cross.

Finally, as Pilate appears, the frenzied mob demands the death of Jesus. At first, Pilate reiterates that the people can have their king and that Barabbas, a rebel accused of leading a murderous insurrection, will never be set free. Caiaphas accuses Pilate of not being Caesar's friend and Annas threatens to inform the Emperor that he gave protection to one guilty of high treason. Among screams of "Crucify him" Pilate gives in to their demands. He announces that the death sentence will be prepared in writing and proclaimed in public, and that Jesus will be crucified with two murderers.

As the sentence is proclaimed, the crosses are brought. The people head for Golgotha – the place of skulls.

Act X – The Way of the Cross – The Crucifixion

Tableau: Isaac, son of Abraham, carries the wood for his own sacrifice up Mount Moriah.

Tableau: Looking at the bronze serpent brings salvation to the Israelites.

Mary, Lazarus and Magdalene wonder why the streets are deserted. John tries to keep Mary from going to Golgotha, but she insists, recalling

Simeon's prophesy when she brought the infant Jesus to the Temple.

To the hate filled scream of the mob, driven with sticks, Jesus staggers up the mountain. He stumbles and falls. The guards drag Jesus along. Mary recognises her son. One of the soldiers forces Simon of Cyrene to carry the cross. Veronica wipes his face. A woman asks, "Rabbi, this is how they reward you?" Jesus asks the women to weep for themselves and their children.

Narrator, soloist & chorus: The cross is raised and Jesus is bound and nailed to the cross.

When Annas sees the raised cross, he is at first delighted, but objects to the inscription, "Jesus the Nazarene, King of the Jews". The priests demand it be torn down but are told that the inscription was attached to the cross by order of the Governor and could not be removed.

Members of the High Council and some of the Roman soldiers taunt Jesus. The soldiers throw dice for his clothing. Jesus asks the Father to forgive them, for they know not what they are doing. His words apply both to Romans and Jews, as well as all of humanity. When one of the robbers asks for mercy from Jesus, he promises that the man will be in paradise that very day. Caiphas and his followers are appalled at Jesus' arrogance.

Mary and John are approaching. Mary prays, "Lord, my God I am suffering agony! Be with me!" Jesus answers, "Woman look at your son! Son, look at your mother!" John promises to honour Mary as his mother and he as her son. Jesus requests a drink and a soldier offers him water. After calling to the Father and commending his spirit to him, Jesus dies. It begins to thunder, the earth quakes, the sun grows dark. Several spectators ask God to have mercy on them. The High Priest is told that the curtain of the Holy of Holies in the Temple has torn.

Mary and Magdalene plead with the soldiers to spare Jesus when they break the bones of the others. After Jesus' side is pierced with a lance and they are sure he is dead, the soldiers consent. They confirm that the body will be given to Joseph of Arimathea by the Governor's consent. Members of the High Council are concerned that the disciples of Jesus

The Way of the Cross

could steal the body and spread the story that he had risen again, as he had prophesised.

John, Magdalene and Mary are mourning. Magdalene reminds them of the words Jesus said when he departed from Bethany: "You will weep and lament... but your sadness will be transformed into joy, and no one will be able to take away your joy." Mary cries out to God.

Chorus

Act XI – The Resurrection

The women enter on their way to the tomb. Magdalene says how happy she is to be able to pay her last respects to her beloved Rabbi. An Angel asks why they are searching for the living among the dead, that he is not here, he has risen from the dead. They enter the tomb and discover it empty save for the burial clothes. Magdalene rejoices: "I know that my saviour lives ... He is with us all the days until the end of the world!... Oh, could I proclaim it

throughout all the worlds, so that the mountains and cliffs and heaven and earth should re-echo with the words:

HALLELUJA! HE IS RISEN!

Concluding meditation – musical selection.

The chorus sings a hymn of praise and jubilation.

INDEX